WITHDRAWN

IF I COULD PREACH
JUST ONCE

IF I COULD PREACH
JUST ONCE

Hon. *Bertrand Russell*

Dr. Joseph Collins

John Drinkwater

G. K. Chesterton

Sheila Kaye-Smith

Sir A. Conan Doyle

Dr. Henry Noble MacCracken

Lord Hugh Cecil

Sir Philip Gibbs

Ludwig Lewisohn

Dr. Henry S. Canby

Prof. J. Arthur Thomson, LL.D.

Sir Thomas Horder

Essay Index Reprint Series

 BOOKS FOR LIBRARIES PRESS
FREEPORT, NEW YORK

Library of Congress Cataloging in Publication Data
Main entry under title:

If I could preach just once.
    (Essay index reprint series)
    CONTENTS: The power of the word, by J. Drinkwater.--
The pagan in the heart, by L. Lewisohn.--The unknown
future, by P. Gibbs. [etc.]
    1. Sermons, English. I. Russell, Hon. Bertrand
Russell, 3d Earl, 1872-1970.
BV4241.I5 1971   252   73-167364
ISBN 0-8369-2457-6

PRINTED IN THE UNITED STATES OF AMERICA
BY
NEW WORLD BOOK MANUFACTURING CO., INC.
HALLANDALE, FLORIDA 33009

CONTENTS

THE POWER OF THE WORD
by John Drinkwater

The Power of the Word

By John Drinkwater

"Who is he that darkeneth counsel by
words without knowledge?"
—Job xxxviii:2.

THERE is a strange illusion in the mind of many
people who pride themselves on being strictly practical that words do not amount to very much. They
are a necessary part of the machinery of business
and affairs and they can be amusing counters in times
of recreation. But when they claim a leading status
in the more serious conduct of the world, this, it is
felt, is going too far. That the pen is mightier than
the sword is by our critics regarded as the extravagance of some heady person, himself a word-
monger. No reproach has a more scathing intent
than to say of a man that he has the gift of the gab,
and the contempt in which the sanguine advocates
of a business government hold the pundits whom

[3]

they would replace, fittingly designates Westminster or Washington as the gasworks.

This may be all very well as preserving the self-esteem of people who find it difficult to say anything about anything, since they have nothing much to say. But it is all very silly. It would not be worth noting if it were not so prevalent and so dangerous. Great numbers of people unhappily do believe that as long as things get done, what is said does not very much matter. They do not realize that it is neither more nor less than as a consequence of what is said that almost everything is done. How profound, and at the same time how obscure, are the operations of this law Shelley knew when he declared that poets were the unacknowledged legislators of the world. The circumstances that govern our life and the happiness or failure that it contains are chiefly the consequence of opinion, and opinion becomes operative only when it is delivered in the word.

Clearly in the economy of our society there is a place for jesting, and a joke is commonly edged by the fact that we do not say precisely what we mean. We may all here allow ourselves what license we will in this respect, so long as we do not too craftily conceal the fact that we are allowing ourselves any license at all. It is not the wit's fault if some dull fellow takes him seriously, but the wit whose notes are, like the bat's, inaudible even to sensitive ears, grows tiresome. But it is not of these more slippered occasions for words that we are speaking. It is rather of the fateful uses to which they are daily put in giving intelligible form to the nebulous thought that inspires and governs all conduct. And the irresponsible view that words do not matter, in placing as it were a sort of outlawry upon them, tends more than anything else to give them the dangerous character of outlaws. Once it is assumed in any society that what is said does not matter it is certain that much will be said that matters disastrously. And so potent do we believe the word to be, that it may be asserted that from its abuse have chiefly sprung the disasters that have befallen civilization.

Most people, I suppose, would say that the first practical problem of this, as indeed of any, age is the preservation of peace. And yet almost every day somebody or another stands up and says that, human nature being what it is, peace cannot be preserved. The speaker always does, or would, add that he himself is all for peace, but that he is a realist and has to face the lamentable imperfections of humanity. The truth is that peace could quite well be preserved, but that it will never be so long as these people go about saying that it cannot. I was talking recently to a friend who takes a responsible part in the work of the League of Nations. I asked him whether after nearly ten years of experience he could candidly say that the League had done much in the accomplishment of its objects. His reply was a very shrewd one. We both agreed with the general view that ten years was in any case an inadequate time for notable results, but, considering that term for what it was worth, he said that he could not claim that the League had been notably successful in any specific enterprise of the first importance, but he added that he was convinced that the continual talk at Geneva about peace had created a general atmosphere in Europe in which it was extremely difficult for any nation to break the peace. That seems to me to be a judgment of the finest discrimination. If today two first-rate powers came to a serious breach, it may be questionable whether the League would be powerful enough in the last resort to restrain them from hostilities. But it is certain if the peace talk at Geneva continues, and if the leaders in all countries who have that crusade most nearly at heart continue to face all skepticism and ridicule as bravely as they have done, that even the great powers will find it increasingly difficult to take up arms in face of the opinion that the words of Geneva are inevitably creating. The machinery of the League may not yet be able to cope with the most serious kind of emergency, but the words of Geneva often enough repeated will make such emergencies less and less likely.

Foremost in our reflections on this topic must be the question of disarmament. If this matter is being discussed by half a dozen people, some one is sure to bring up the stale argument that it would be suicidal for us, or any other nation, to disarm without a common compact. This view always flies at once to the head of any firebrand present, and he will not only insist upon the necessity of full equipment, but tell you how and where the next war will break out. The talk of independent disarmament is nonsense because everybody knows that there is not the smallest possibility of any power, great or small, venturing upon such a policy. The only hope for any serious disarmament program is that it shall be undertaken by that same mutual compact, but it is precisely the menace of the firebrand's irresponsible words that makes the compact so difficult to realize. To these dangerous abuses of words I would throw out a direct challenge. When such a one stands up and proclaims war as being inevitable, I would say to him that in his heart he wants war. It is no use for him to tell me that he does not want it, but that other people do. Who, may I ask, are the other people who do, if they are not those who, like himself, are speaking dangerously to the world? If you preach war, you will have war. If you preach peace, you will have peace. Since it is not to be supposed that all men will preach the same thing at the same time, it follows that you will have war or peace as the greater number preach the one or the other. And every man who preaches war is preparing war. To do this in the name of patriotism seems to me to be the most inexcusable kind of cowardice. There are, in fact, in the world a few people who are born fighters and who are never really happy unless there is a fight on. When they preach war I can respect them. But I can respect no others who preach it, for it is they and they alone who are making probable a calamity which they profess to deplore.

Here, clearly, is a matter of supreme importance

in which what is said is of the greatest consequence. Any word irresponsibly spoken is a betrayal of humanity. Let us suppose, for example, that every effective state in the world were represented by one of its most authoritative leaders at Geneva. And suppose that in a time of international difficulties, which in these days almost inevitably affect the civilized organism as a whole, these accredited leaders said with one voice that they thought war to be an unthinkable solution, that there should be no war. Would any one of them lack the overwhelming support of the people behind them at home? In such a situation there could be no rhetorical question of national honor. Not having the stoical fortitude of a Quaker, if I quarrel with somebody and he hits me, I shall probably hit him back if I can. I should even see some point in a charge of pusillanimity if I failed to do so. But if in our quarrel we both from the outset are determined that whatever happens we will not hit each other, I know of no sophism which could convince me that we either of us suffer loss of honor. And if our representative statesmen firmly took up the position that I have indicated when occasion arose, there could then be no such question, either. It is fair to say that the great majority of responsible leaders in the world at this moment believe that such an attitude would be a right and courageous one, but the danger is that each one of them might be kept from saying so in council by a fear that the others would say nothing of the sort. The fear, in the light of any psychological understanding, is misconceived. A clear lead given by a very small minority in such a contingency, speaking with the prestige of national authority, would almost certainly be followed by the majority. And the surest way of encouraging responsible leaders to such witness is for all of us, the people whom they represent, to preach peace always and war never. Every time that the supposed inevitability of war is asserted, even in a private conversation, something is done to weaken the spirit by which alone war can be made possible. I do not propose to mention any names on this occasion, but it has always seemed to me that the bravest soldier of our time is a man who is not only distinguished by a long career of the greatest gallantry in the field, but who has without fear of consequences to himself not only said consistently in public that war is a horrible thing that ought to be outlawed, but has as consistently encouraged a belief that it can be outlawed.

Another matter in which the use of the word is today of high importance is the relations between Great Britain and the United States. These relations are obviously full of delicacies that need always careful adjustment. They are complicated by the fact that, having a common language, the people of the two countries are apt to think that they know each other a good deal better than they do. If you are with a man who knows nothing of your language, as you know nothing of his, while you will not understand him, you also will not misunderstand him; but if you are talking to a man whose language seems to be your own and yet to a man whose national habits and institutions and ideals and manners are in many respects not your own at all, there is manifestly a danger of frequent confusion. And from this confusion spring many hasty and ill-founded judgments which, irresponsibly spoken, are full of danger. Nevertheless, a sympathetic understanding between Great Britain and America is as possible as it plainly is desirable for the welfare of humanity. And here again what is said, even in private conversation, does very much matter. A little superficial knowledge which can be more readily picked up between the peoples of these countries than between

[11]

those of any others, is a great provoker of the slightly pondered word. The easy exchange of speech leads us to as easy an assumption of exhaustive information. The Londoner who spends a fortnight in New York with a couple of days in Boston and perhaps a couple in Chicago, or the New Yorker who has been a week in London and an hour or two in Oxford and Stratford-on-Avon, has, with his facilities of language, learned so much that he is apt to flatter himself that he has learned all. And since some of the things that he has learned vex and puzzle him, he may become a very dangerous false prophet. "Who is he that darkeneth counsel by words without knowledge?" I happen myself to have spent rather a considerable time in America, and I have found many things to bewilder me there. But I never speak about them unless I am chaffing some of my own best American friends, where I know no offense can be given or taken. On the other hand, I have found there much of enlightenment and sympathy, and these seem to me to be things immensely more significant and worthy of report. For here again, if you preach friction, you will have friction, and if you preach friendship, you will have friendship. There is no question of evading specific difficulties or of affecting to admire things that you dislike. These upon their occasions have to be debated openly. But their occasions need be no more than the differences that at times have to be composed between friends anywhere. In general terms, those of us who care for Anglo-American good will, and see in it an instrument of incalculable power, should let that good will guide the word. Witty impatience and angry impatience alike are in this matter dangerous to the commonweal. It is now a century and a half since it was determined that America and Britain should be two nations, and the sentimental pretense that in some sort of way they are still one does nothing to engender the respect upon which alone international understanding can be founded. But because of certain common traditions of ancestry and speech and government there is an opportunity, if it could be taken, of an understanding existing here such as has hardly been known before between two great countries in history. The example might do more than anything else to make straight many of the crooked ways of our civilization. And again, it is an example that must be realized by a steadily responsible use of the word. It is time that we all of us dropped the superstition that what is said does not matter. For, once a thing was said that does profoundly matter to us all—"But I say unto you, that every idle word that men shall speak, they shall give account thereof in the day of judgment."

THE PAGAN IN THE HEART

by Ludwig Lewisohn

The Pagan in the Heart

By Ludwig Lewisohn

I

IT IS many years since I heard a sermon. But since all that I ever heard began with a text, I am glad to avail myself, too, of that agreeable method which gives one so natural a starting point. I choose my text, then, from a very ancient book, from that famous Talmudic tractate known as the Sayings or Sentences of the Fathers which has quite generally been embodied in the liturgy of the synagogue. And in this book I select the whole of the brief eighteenth section of the first chapter. It reads as follows: "Rabban Shimon ben Gamaliel was wont to say, It is upon three things that the world stands firm—upon justice, upon truth and upon peace." This saying of our teacher Simeon, the son of that patriarch Gamaliel who was the instructor of the young Saul of Tarsus, may not, at first sight, seem either

[17]

very astonishing or very original. But to translate is notoriously to traduce; there are no synonyms; the names of concepts in one language do not coincide with the apparently same names in another. For concepts are freighted with the peculiar character and experience of the particular people who sum up in them their unique vision of the multiform world. Hence, like a preacher in those far days when people were not ashamed of knowledge, I may be permitted to say that the original words for "upon justice and truth and upon peace are, *Al-hadin v'al-haemeth v'al-hashalom."* In brief, the Hebrew words translated as justice, truth, and peace are *din, emeth* and *shalom,* and it is these words that may be fruitfully examined for a moment.

Din is no "Justice with her scales in bronze," no blindfold Roman effigy, no symbol of a power that stands unmoved above humanity and measures it by some cold and abstract norm. The verbal stem from which the noun derives means to create right, balance, equity among men, to use mercy and to abstain from the judging that destroys justice. It is the word used by Isaiah when he declares that Javeh will enter into judgment with the elders and princes of the folk because the spoil of the poor is in their

[18]

houses; it is the word used by Jeremiah concerning the king Josiah: "He judged the cause of the poor and needy; then it was well. Was not this to know me, saith Javeh?" . . . This justice on which the world is founded leans always to the side of the defeated, the disinherited; it is exercised in creating a moral balance of which the natural world does not know. . . .

Precisely as *din* is no pagan justice that wreaks itself upon life in the name of some arrogant law, so *emeth* (truth) is not the name of a metaphysical concept. This truth is that which shall endure, all that has steadfastness and faithfulness—the ultimate values upon which all men can rely in their souls' last need. It is, according to the prophets, inseparable from peace; it is, according to the Psalmist, inseparable from love: *Chesed v'emeth,* loving-kindness and truth. It is the name of God—*El emeth,* his stamp and seal. It is the cognizance whereby love can actively create peace. And this peace —*shalom* —of which justice and truth, equity and steadfastness, are the conditions, is also spiritual health, the welfare of the total man, salvation. Peace is salvation in the view of my text, not redemption—*p'duth* —ransoming, buying off. For according to the author of my text there exists neither original taint nor unforgivable sin. Mercy and truth will bring about the salvation whose name is peace.

II

It will be said that, despite the special interpretation, these are commonplaces and that I have quite correctly compared myself to an old-fashioned preacher. But there are, in fact, no new ethics under the sun; there is no new road to human salvation, and I observe that the most extreme of modern moral nihilists, like Mr. Aldous Huxley, for example, pay their implicit and half shamefaced tribute to that Jewish wisdom which failed as Christianity through its contamination with pagan mysticism and emotion and through its gradual implication with the power of Rome.

There is no new wisdom of the humanistic sort, of the sort that teaches men how to live. There was a moment in the nineteenth century when it was hoped that science would provide a new ethic. That hope is dead. Science is doing untold good in sanitating the lives of the already intelligent and merciful. One thinks, for instance, of the safer practice of contraception, of the early but already amazing triumphs of endocrinology. But science cannot make men merciful. On the contrary, it puts into the hands of the pagan—the ruthless industrialist, the mad nationalist, the professional militarist—engines of power that would have made Rome shudder. New poison gases can subdue striking workers and wipe out civilian populations. The military despotisms of the world are more secure than ever; the dictator buys the man in the laboratory; those two enter into a desperate league. Science triumphs; death and not life is king; the heart has not been touched; salvation is farther off than ever.

The heart has not been touched. Or to speak with an at least apparently greater precision: there has not been, so far as one can see, the slightest emotional adjustment to the ethic which Christendom feigns to accept. Whenever European pagans have seemed to make such an adjustment they have robbed their example of all saving power by their monkish perversity, their repudiation of man and nature and human life, their repulsive morbidness. Neither Saint Francis kissing the sores of lepers nor the aged and satiated Tolstoi thundering against art and love can help us. Our duty toward lepers is to eliminate their disease; by art and love we live. The pagan, in other words, alternates between truculence and groveling, between excess and emasculation, drunkenness and the Volstead Act, exposing sickly babies on mountain ledges or letting them be born indiscriminately. He never touches the center. He never touches justice, truth, and peace.

It is for this reason that, through my text, I appealed to Jewish ethics, that is to say, to Christian ethics untainted by pagan psychology, by its excesses, by its lust for superiority and power. The author of my text, Simeon, the son of the patriarch Gamaliel, and his predecessors to Amos, the earliest of the prophets, and his successors to any intelligent, unfashionable rabbi in Lemberg or Kansas City, represent an entirely different, a strictly non-pagan attitude to human life. Profoundly, sincerely, instinctively, not only as a matter of so-called religious conviction but of rock-founded common sense and unalterable experience these men have believed and believe that the senses are legitimate, that human life is manageable, that force is absolutely and undeviatingly evil, and that salvation arises naturally, without the interposition of mythical intermediary or metaphysical balderdash, by that tireless and loving coöperation among the children of Adam whose end and aim and fruit are peace. When huge Oriental monarchies threatened the national existence of their people, these men counseled defeat and exile rather than resistance; when Hadrian forbade by ruthless edicts all the immemorial practices of the Jewish cult, there was found but one man in the assembly of sages to countenance the armed resistance under Bar Kochba. The others practiced a non-resistant disobedience. They were aware then, in the first quarter of the second century of our era, that to meet force with force and paganism with paganism was only to put off all hope of the reign of justice, truth, and peace.

What, in brief, I am trying to point out is that there exists and has long existed in our Western World and not only among quietistic Hindus on the path to Nirvana, the psychology, the emotional attitude that alone—alone—can save the civilization we have built up. I shall not say with Spengler that according to a law inherent in the morphology of all civilizations we are doomed to a Babylonian fate whatever we attempt or do. But that intolerable and bloody Cæsarian age which he predicts may in truth come upon us unless we can eliminate not only arms and guns and navies and the recurrent call to military servitude, but the primitive pagan emotions that render all these inevitable. Disarmament conferences, multilateral peace-treaties—all these will be vain and empty unless the emotional attitude of John Smith can be so changed that he will say, when war looms, what Moses Levy finds burning on his lips but does not dare to say: Fighting is dirty, sinful, and unworthy of man. Above all it is immeasurably stupid; it settles nothing; it is suicidal for all concerned. It is absolute evil as well as absolute stupidity. That is why Moses Levy, even when he follows the drum in fear of being lynched, has an essential contempt both for those who beat the drum and for those who follow it gladly.

What shall we do to change the inner man of John Smith? How shall we make him want justice, truth, peace? How shall we persuade him not to follow the call to murder and destroy whether that call is issued by a capitalist or a proletarian dictatorship? How? By lifting from him the burden of his littleness, of his fear. For he is cruel because he is afraid

[24]

of being hurt and he plunges into mass emotion and mass obedience and mass murder because that plunge gives him a sense of power, the power of the mass to which he belongs and which he briefly feels to be his own. Especially in our modern urban and industrialist civilization when he has been so hopelessly reduced to a cipher. Feebly he brags and boasts out of his insignificance and his fears. Put a uniform on him and make him part of the wheeling evolutions of a military mass. He feels upheld, sustained, proud in obedience and uniformity, powerful with the power of at last being and not only tending a part of a machine. . . .

Doubtless in sodden trenches under gunfire this false sense of power abandons him and he would like to whimper and to flee. But now the solidarity of common danger keeps him somewhat erect; he does not know how uselessly and stupidly it was incurred, and also the old pagan superstition—useful perhaps in primitive ages but now no more—that it is shameful for a man to fear physical hurt. And Christianity with its silly contempt for the body has left him utterly pagan in this respect. The regimentation of the industrialized master-state, aided

[25]

by church and school and the excesses of moralistic feminism, reduces poor Smith's virile expressiveness in work, in play, in love below a tolerable minimum. He roars for the flag and feels elated; he sees battleships maneuver and feels their gray strength added to his pitiful weakness. The oligarchs know how to take him and how to turn him into cannonfodder. Then when pain and danger come the poor fellow is helpless. In his childhood he was fed on stories of Indians bearing torture without a complaint and was taught that this poor quality of the Stone Age savage was worthy of imitation, was in fact the very mark and sign of manhood. And in his instruction in school and Sunday school the Jew Jesus is transformed for him as far as possible into a Nordic knight, not a gentle man but a gentleman or, in America—*vide* Bruce Barton—into a go-getting man of business like the boss of his concern. Belligerency is bred into the very bone and marrow of poor John Smith, but never a belligerency for his minimum rights to freedom, love, play, sunlight, but belligerency for a flag, a figment, a vision of fancied danger and unnecessary solidarity behind which crouch his masters, who send him to prison if he criticizes the mad system by which he is enslaved

[26]

and ordered into trenches to protect the sources of
their power.

III

Perhaps it will be possible some day to drive from
John Smith's heart the servile pagan ideal with which
it has been corrupted for so many ages. Perhaps
from a henchman he can be turned into a man. The
cults of the Far East are useless to us, for we need
more insistence on the dignity and preciousness of
personality, not less; more respect for healthy and
beautiful bodies, and not less. Historical Christianity will not help us in any of its forms, for all these
forms are inextricably entangled with the world's
pomp and power, with patriotism and force. And
even a quite pure faith like that of the Quakers is
contaminated by the morbid asceticism of Paul. This
is a central point and this the central tragedy of
Christianity, that it has never been able to strive for
the salvation of peace without demanding at the
same time a disgusting monkishness of conduct. Its
peace has always been peace for the sake of death,
never peace for the sake of a more abundant life.
Cannot we persuade John Smith that not to judge,

[27]

that to prefer truth to propaganda and to seek peace may be a manly and an honorable way of life?

He will not take kindly to regarding for his own benefit the operations of the mind and heart of Moses Levy. Ages of prejudice and slander forbid that. But those who know that on John Smith's putting on a new man depends the salvation of the world—it is they who may be brought to regard Moses Levy with an at least objective and scientific interest. Now Moses Levy has had an historic experience so recurrent and profound that it has turned into an instinct of his blood the truth that an appeal to force settles nothing at all. He despises all values except moral and intellectual values. If he sees two men fighting his contempt for the victor and the defeated is precisely the same. His contempt is softened by a single consideration: the defeated was probably, or at least possibly, in the right. So that injustice, which he finds of all things hardest to bear, has been added to dirt and brutality. He has himself become a pretty poor creature as far as action is concerned. John Smith has bawled "coward" at him so long that instead of saying, "In your precise sense I am, thank God, a coward," he has mimicked the courage of John Smith as a self-protective gesture and has furnished examples of gallantry in every modern war. But it has always been against the grain of his nature; it has always been a horrible and costly gesture. Levy believes in peace and does not think it a fine thing to be hurt or maimed or to incur the danger of it, and always has the shrewdest of suspicions that the quarrels he is asked to enter are not his quarrels or those of any of his ordinary fellow men at all. Furthermore, in Levy's consciousness—here is his great advantage—peace has never been entangled with a repudiation of nature; it has, on the contrary, been implicated with a resistless love of life. He is no monkish or Tolstoian lover of peace and barrenness. He is passionate son and husband and father. If his wife's or his child's or his own finger aches he runs to his physician. He loathes the thought of hurt, of death, of war, of confusion. He loves life and peace, food and drink, music and sunshine, study and reflection. The dead or the embattled have none of these. In a thousand pogroms he has shown that he can bear the inevitable with dignity. But he gets no "kick" out of contention and danger. That pagan possibility has completely died out of his nature. He wants literally and passionately to be left in peace in order to pursue the goods which seem to him the true goods of human life: love, children, knowledge, charity, good health, old age.

He often seems contemptible to John Smith. The mimic battles of Smith's games, Smith's pseudo-knightly ideals and gestures, are not for him. He is serious; he reckons with reality. He has been up against reality a long, long time. He sometimes, in the light of Smith's apparently gay, brave world, feels a trifle contemptuous of himself. Smith runs amok or kills himself; Levy sighs and goes to a psychoanalyst. Smith has all the fine gestures; Levy manages to conquer life. For Levy never experienced the knightly tradition or the Christian Middle Ages. Abstract sociological loyalties play no part in his life. He is not thrilled by the flutter of any flag nor taken in by any symbol. Life is too serious and too dangerous for that. He does not want his sons to be killed, however handsome the name of the cause. He wants them to live and be healthy and learned and to beget sons in their turn even more healthy and learned, and in this thought is his final affirmation of humanity as well as his share of immortality. He is eager to practice charity, for pain and want hurt and he does not think that being hurt is either a fine thing or a discipline; he has an infinite respect for the best truth he can find, being rarely taken in by quackery of any sort, but relying on science; he wants peace above all things, peace without which none of the ends of the good life can be served.

IV

Paganism must be curbed, the knightly and the loyal must be put to useful work, the serious and the cowards must prevail in the councils of mankind. The danger is great and imminent. Civilization is on a knife's edge. Does no one want to save it? A little humble anti-Fascist fled from Italy, an un-political person, a man who quietly wanted to with-draw from the degradations of a tyrant. He came to France, home of exiles and last refuge of the op-pressed, and month in and month out begged and besought the Italian consul in Paris to permit his wife and child to join him. In vain. In vain. The little man lost his head and fired on the consul. A French jury, deeply cognizant of the man's wrongs and sufferings, let him off with a sentence of two years. Now armed guards are needed by the French consulates in Italy and Mussolini talks of national insult and provocation to war. Here are all the makings of a second Sarajevo. For Italy is allied with the bloody despotisms of Poland, Hungary, and Rumania. And it will do us no good, if war comes, to feel a passionate sympathy for France. For war destroys and brutalizes all. There are not in the moral and hardly in the physical sense either conquerors or conquered. All go down to disaster, disgrace, destruction, despair. All. Force, honor, prestige, even fatherland—these are murderous concepts and murderous things, pagan, horrible, tragic. If John Smith does not learn from the despised Moses Levy civilization is doomed.

For we must never forget that in John Smith is our only hope. I must not say that none among his rulers in any country has the will to good and to peace. But that will can never or hardly ever be liberated from its entanglement with power, gear, friendship, ultimate class solidarity. It is hard for a Senator's son to become a conscientious objector to military slavery and official murder. He who has least to lose is the free man. But he must be made to realize his freedom; he must refuse to be dazzled by symbols, scared by false cries of danger, confused by the figment of a concept of honor that lost all meaning centuries ago. His conversion is not an easy task. For John Smith has through the ages been tribesman, feudal vassal, loyal subject, one-hundred-per-cent citizen—everything, in fact, except a human being. He has always been the object of the processes of history. Is there any hope of converting him at this late date into a man?

I think there is; I hope there is. For I do not believe that in his innermost soul he is so very different from Moses Levy. Only his historic experience has been an unhappier one. He has been fooled into thinking himself a conqueror. He has warped memories. If he is a Frenchman he thinks, let us say, in terms of the splendor of Napoleon, not in terms of his great-great grandfather, who probably drowned miserably in the icy waters of the Beresina or froze to death on the wintry Russian plains. Moses Levy has the felicity of realistically thinking in terms of his grandfather, of his great-grandfather; he is not fooled by a splendid memory and a name still graven above a palace door. He knows what the world is really like. Now at bottom John Smith, quite like Moses Levy, probably wants love, children, knowledge, peace. Being an Aryan and a natural pagan and young in the discipline of history, he probably, unlike Moses Levy in this respect, still has a hankering for what he calls victory—some primitive desire, stripped of any moral motive or aim, to prevail, to create a superiority he does not feel by, at least symbolically, getting his knee upon some rival tribesman's chest. Can we not teach him that no victory is his or ever has been and that, closely regarded, such a thing as victory is no longer possible in a crowded and complicated world? Even the shadow of victory works by contraries. It is the Italian master who is becoming corrupted, brutalized, degraded in the South Tyrol; it is the Tyrolese who will some day arise from their sufferings erect, spiritually purged, lovers of justice and of peace.

Nothing will save us except peace. Economic and social justice, humanitarian endeavor, scientific discoveries—all are vain if destruction and utter degradation are always just around the corner. We must go out into the world; we must go to John Smith and drive the pagan from his heart—the foolish, short-sighted, self-destructive pagan. We must be tireless in this aim until a day comes when, if the masters call to war, no one answers the call, but men, quietly disregarding flag and drum and the paid lies of the press, go about their business of peace. And we can still go to John Smith, not only in the name of his essential manhood and his posterity, but in the name of Jesus. Not of Christ. Christ is a knight and a gentleman and a pagan myth. But in the name of Jesus and the teachers of Jesus and the descendants of those teachers who are still many among the kinsmen of the Nazarene. For nearly two-thousand years these men have known that peace alone is salvation. Upon justice and truth and peace our world rests. The pagan has raged against these pillars of the world for ages. They are near to toppling. We must save them and so ourselves and our world from crumbling back into chaos.

THE UNKNOWN FUTURE
by Sir Philip Gibbs

The Unknown Future

By Sir Philip Gibbs

STRANGE things are happening in the world today, though we are almost unaware of their significance because they are happening in the hidden, or unconscious, mind of humanity. Radical changes in the conditions and problems of life are coming close to us as every day passes towards an unknown future. But we are not as yet prepared for them with any philosophy or faith which might enable us to direct our own destiny.

The traditions by which our fathers shaped their lives have been challenged and shaken. Their ideals are now for the most part rejected and despised. The faith which reconciled them in some measure with life itself, and gave them courage to face death with hope in spiritual survival, has lost its authority in many minds. They are not reconciled with this life or that death, but desperately unsatisfied, bewildered, and uncertain.

[39]

The old moralities seem mere foolishness now to many of our younger people who are testing every ancient law by new experience with a rash but rather splendid courage, as though they were new Adams and Eves without any past or any guidance. The present phase of civilization is ending, as a new page is turned over in the book of life. It is passing from us before our eyes, though many do not see. In a little while it will have been replaced by something else—better or worse. Who knows?

The world war had something to do with this, though not everything. That conflict of nations destroyed more than empires and cities and cathedrals and irreplaceable life. It destroyed something in the mind of the world—belief in the old leadership and ideals. It shocked for a time all faith in any kind of authority. Millions of men who had gone into the zone of fire with exalted heroism and self-sacrifice, under the spell of passionate emotion, believing that by their service humanity would reach greater heights of justice—with more generous rewards and more certain security for the common man who had revealed his nobility in all this agony —returned in disillusion and despair and felt themselves betrayed. So many ideals went down in mud and blood. So many promises were unfulfilled. So many men thought out things anew, and denied everything they had once believed. So many were shell-shocked. Was not the whole world shell-shocked in those dreadful years, and afterward?

A younger crowd, born in the shadow of the war, have escaped altogether from that darkness, but many of them reject the past which led up to that conflict with a kind of laughing contempt for the folly of their fathers—even for their heroism in such a cause—and for most of the enthusiasms, emotions, and traditions which belonged to the heritage of the human mind before the war. Can one blame them, looking back at recent history?

Youth will have nothing of the past. It is not much interested in the past, except for a smiling wonderment that such things should have been and that men and women should have thought that way. It has rejected much of its heritage as only fit for lumber rooms of rubbish, careless of many treasures there. It is conscious only of its own vitality and needs. It is not afraid of new adventure. But many of these younger minds are restless and discontented with their present state, curious, but uncertain and

[41]

cynical, of life's meaning and purpose, if there is any meaning.

This break with the past was only partly caused by the war. The rapid advance of scientific discovery has broken down the old framework of human thought. Hardly a day passes and never a year without some new revelation or achievement by the scientists, giving us more understanding and control of certain forces. Less than a hundred years ago the social habits of many nations were completely changed by the application of steam to mechanical energy. Now greater changes will happen—are happening—with increased velocity. They will alter, surely, the whole system and structure of human society. The old rhythm of life, so quiet and leisurely for thousands of years, has altered its beat. It is moving to a faster measure and its pace is accelerating. Physically we may move about the world with increasing rapidity. Every month, almost, records are broken in the speed of travel. The victory of flight has not yet achieved its full and universal triumph.

In a little while, beyond all doubt, flying will become a safe and normal way of transport. The sky will be crowded with traffic, crossing and recrossing the frontiers of nations, making the world smaller when measured by time, bringing people closer together as friends, or—if their minds do not move so quickly as machines—as enemies.

When that happens our cities and streets will be built upon a different kind of plan and the very outward aspect of life will be changed from what is now familiar to us.

Science is also speeding up the transmission of thought and breaking down the barriers between one mind and another. All those vibrations of light and sound which have been harnessed lately to new instruments are only beginning to touch the massed intelligence of human beings. That delicate mechanism which enables us to speak to the far ends of the earth, and soon will let us see across the world, may seem to us now only the exhibition of wonder-working toys, a little boring when their novelty has passed. But such new powers must alter somehow the minds of men and women. Humanity with those means of communication, as quick as thought itself, far reaching, cannot remain the same as when small communities had but a narrow range of interest and ideas, extending farther, or not easily, beyond their own frontiers. Presently all the peoples of the world will be talking to one another, looking at one another, calling to one another, by that invisible energy which brings all space into a back parlor.

This modern science holds out high promises to humanity if the knowledge that is coming to us is rightly used. We are in command already of vast powers which may be directed to the relief of human labor and to the ease and beauty of life. More power, exceeding perhaps anything we have yet known, by enabling us to get hold of the very sources of energy as it is stored up in the universe or in the atom, may one day be ours. In any case our present knowledge is sufficient to produce a material prosperity and a mechanical activity—not yet evenly distributed or fully developed—which would have seemed miraculous half a century ago, but has no imaginable limit.

Biologists and chemists offer mankind new hopes of eliminating disease, increasing the span of life and extending the period of youth. Psychologists, probing into the secrets of the mind and discovering its influence over the body, hint at the possibility of developing mental faculties which would give man more mastery over life and death.

Splendid promises! In the light of them the future looks bright. And yet, alas! they suggest new dangers as well as new hopes. It is not yet certain that the next phase of history which is advancing so rapidly will see any progress in human happiness. It is indeed not yet certain that this civilization of ours—by no means perfect, but with certain values of beauty and knowledge and nobility—will not go down in some great catastrophe.

The truth is—and we must face it—that we are in possession of powers which may lead to our own destruction, and that all this speeding up of the rhythm of life may be a rush forward to ruin. We are building up a mechanical activity which may overmaster humanity itself by making machines more important than men. We are inventing engines which may be turned against ourselves. The minds of men are not keeping pace with the power which is now in their hands.

The last war, in spite of all its heroism among common men, was a frightful revelation of our low standard of intelligence and morality, especially among those who were the leaders and rulers of the world. The victory of flight had only just been won as the fulfillment of an age-long dream which might give a new touch of divinity—the liberty of the skies—to earth-bound men, but it was used as an instrument of death, not sparing even women and children in crowded cities. In that war all the knowledge given to us by science, the genius of physicists and chemists, the research of the world's greatest brains probing into the mysteries of nature, were devoted to the purpose of destroying human life, by high explosives, by poison gas, by long-range guns, by delicate and deadly machines, made with a skill which God might praise as handicraft if used for any other purpose. Since then our knowledge has advanced. Since then—only ten years ago—we know how to kill each other far more efficiently. Bigger bombs may be dropped from faster airplanes. Guns have increased their range. Transport has been mechanized. Chemists have invented poison gases far more noxious. Those vibrations which enable thought to travel swiftly by light and sound may be converted to the use of the destroyer. They may control and set in motion ingenious instruments for the destruction of human life and the cities in which it dwells most densely. They may send out the signals of another world war from which Western civilization at least will not escape next time. For it seems likely that if the white races who defend the last heritage of Christendom tear themselves to pieces once again, and use the powers which science has given them with an efficiency which would make the last war seem old-fashioned and humane, then other races will be ready to advance across the ruins.

There are other dangers ahead, not so obvious, but leading to weakness and defeat. No civilization has yet survived after the downfall of its gods. Its doom is declared when the faith and idealism which formed the basis of its laws, the inspiration of its art, and the meaning of its life are challenged by skepticism, and then abandoned in disbelief. Some other and better civilization may take its place, or it may lie buried and forgotten in jungles where its ancient monuments are hidden in the under-growth.

Such skepticism and unbelief are now undermining the foundation of European civilization as it was built up on Christian ideals—often violated, never fulfilled, a thousand times betrayed—but permeating its laws, its art, its emotions, and its discipline.

Not science, but the misunderstanding and false interpretation of science, has caused this spreading skepticism, and in many minds a complete denial of the faith out of which our civilization grew. As the physical laws and mechanism of life in all its forms and activities are revealed more clearly, the modern mind, rushing to wrong conclusions, is losing its belief in spiritual values and ideas. The greatest scientists are not to blame for this. On the contrary, they warn us that all their knowledge leads only to other mysteries and that their discoveries do not reach out to the infinite truth beyond, which is undiscovered and undiscoverable by scientific methods. But that warning is hardly heard in the market place where the cheapjacks of knowledge sell their falsities and where the mass mind is dazzled and excited by mechanical toys. It seems to many students of sensationalized science that chemistry disproves morality by asserting that instincts and passions may be affected or changed by a little doctoring with the ductless glands. They are tempted to believe that science denies God, that personality does not survive after death, that self-discipline is merely foolishness because the mind of man is but an expression of animal behaviorism and all ideas no more than chemical reactions to physical stimuli. So arguing from half knowledge spread about the world in little text-books, their logic is unanswerable and one understands the cause of so much fretfulness and so much materialism in revolt against the ideals of past ages and the old moralities. "If," they say, "there is no future life, let us get all we can here and now, by any kind of means. If morality is only a physiological affair, then let us go to the chemists and get rid of conscience. If there is no God or any future judgment of present acts, let us desert our wives if we tire of them, let us prevent childbirth to save worry and expense, let us grab what we can and have a good time somehow, because tomorrow we die and all is done."

Such ideas are at work in the world today. They are being put to the test, not with much success or happiness. They are more dangerous to our civilization than war itself, because they will lead to an anarchy which is worse than war, and will disintegrate society as effectively as high explosives and with the aid of them. For nations holding that view of life will not be careful of morality, nor of charity, nor of any ideal beyond self-interest. They will try to grab what they want while the grabbing is good.

Those are the dangers we have to face. They are not imaginary, nor the morbid prophecies of pessimistic minds, nor the sensationalism of Sunday journalists. The conflict is already in progress between those who believe in spiritual values and those who deny them. It began, indeed, in the minds of the first men and women because it is the old struggle between good and evil and between selfishness and idealism. But now another crisis is coming in that long-drawn battle, because of this rapid advance of mechanical progress, and the discovery of those new powers which men may use to destroy those who disagree with them.

At all costs we must reëstablish faith in spiritual values. Somehow we must believe in God or go to the devil. We must worship something beyond ourselves lest we destroy ourselves.

We cannot go back in history, dragging out old fetishes which once put a spell upon the human mind. We cannot even return by will power to that simplicity of mind which existed before the age of science. We cannot isolate ourselves from the spirit of the time. It would be folly to do so. We must go forward, not denying science—there is no need to deny it—but using it as a new proof of faith, to build a bridge across the great chasm between knowledge and mystery, and time and eternity. We need, not less science, but more science to understand values beyond analysis, and to be more wor-

[50]

shipful of truth and power beyond our intellectual limitations. We must readapt our minds to new conditions, not afraid of change yet never abandoning those spiritual realities which belong to history and tradition. They are not old and outworn, because truth has no age, and the spirit that moves through the endless adventure of life is forever young.

In our own country and our own race we have a heritage of tradition, a spiritual continuity of law and order, and a love of good and noble things, revealed in the lives and work of countless men and women, which we cannot abandon without enormous loss. It is indeed in our blood and hearts, and we could not cut it out and stay alive as a nation or a race. We must reach back to our past for those values while moving forward to the future, for we shall need those qualities, and not any different ones, to meet the next adventure as we have met life always with a certain cheerful confidence and a sturdy sense of humor, and courage that did not fail at a crisis. Youth has no use for the past, it says, but the past directs them to their destiny. This race of ours, so spread about the world, has in many ways the decision of the future. What we make of life

[51]

will be largely what the world will make of life. Our faith today will make the history of tomorrow.

We need no new faith, but a reassertion of ideals which for a time have weakened, in the modern mind, and a closer fellowship with all peoples who share them with us. Those dangers ahead—that world war—need not happen—nor will ever happen —if we use the powers that have been given us not for death but for life.

With faith again in a divine love beyond the rivalries of men we may disarm the powers of evil. The destroyer will not get his chance if we have a sense of comradeship with other peoples, widening our sympathies beyond national selfishness. We need not use poison gas, nor see great cities smashed by high explosives, if we give a lead to the world in the quest of beauty and truth. Let us love laughter and tolerance and good-fellowship. Let us hate cruelty. Let us have courage to face up to life, whatever it brings, and scorn the grossness that suffocates the soul.

Throughout all the struggles and strivings of our race, all its blunderings and conflicts, all its stupidities and failures, those ideals lived in many simple and noble minds, and that faith helped us through.

[52]

Only by such faith again, reawakened, strengthened by science, reaching out across the world, controlling the machines and instruments of power, working for peace and raising the standard of charity, in the spirit of Christ, may we go forward to meet the unknown future, unafraid.

LUCIFER, OR THE ROOT OF EVIL
by *G. K. Chesterton*

Lucifer, or the Root of Evil

By G. K. Chesterton

IF I had only one sermon to preach, it would be a sermon against pride. The more I see of existence, and especially of modern practical and experimental existence, the more I am convinced of the reality of the old religious thesis: that all evil began with some attempt at superiority; some moment when, as we might say, the very skies were cracked across like a mirror, because there was a sneer in heaven.

Now the first fact to note about this notion is a rather curious one. Of all such notions, it is the one most generally dismissed in theory and most universally accepted in practice. Modern men imagine that such a theological idea is quite remote from them; and stated as a theological idea, it probably is remote from them. But as a matter of fact, it is too close to them to be recognized. It is so completely a part of their minds and morals and instincts, I might almost say of their bodies, that they take it for granted and act on it even before they think of it. It is actually the most popular of all moral ideas; and yet it is almost entirely unknown as a moral idea. No truth is now so unfamiliar as a truth, or so familiar as a fact.

Let us put the fact to a trifling but not unpleasing test. Let us suppose that the reader, or (preferably) the writer, is going into a public house or some public place of social intercourse; a public tube or tram might do as well, except that it seldom allows of such long and philosophical intercourse as did the old public house. Anyhow, let us suppose any place where men of motley but ordinary types assemble; mostly poor because the majority are poor, some moderately comfortable but what is rather snobbishly called common; an average handful of human beings. Let us suppose that the inquirer, politely approaching this group, opens the conversation in a chatty way by saying, "Theologians are of opinion that it was one of the superior angelic intelligences seeking to become the supreme object of worship, instead of finding his natural joy in worshiping, which dislocated the providential design and frustrated the full joy and completion of the cosmos." After making these remarks the inquirer will gaze

[58]

round brightly and expectantly at the company for corroboration, at the same time ordering such refreshments as may be ritually fitted to the place or time, or perhaps merely offering cigarettes or cigars to the whole company, to fortify them against the strain. In any case, we may well admit that such a company will find it something of a strain to accept the formula in the above form. Their comments will probably be disjointed and detached; whether they take the form of "Lorlumme" (a beautiful thought slurred somewhat in pronunciation) or even "Gorblime" (an image more somber but fortunately more obscure) or merely the unaffected form of "Garn"; a statement quite free from doctrinal and denominational teaching, like our state compulsory education. In short, he who shall attempt to state this theory, as a theory, to the average crowd of the populace, will doubtless find that he is talking in an unfamiliar language. Even if he states the matter in the simplified form, that pride is the worst of the seven deadly sins, he will only produce a vague and rather unfavorable impression that he is preaching. But he is only preaching what everybody else is practicing; or at least is wanting everybody else to practice.

Let the scientific inquirer continue to cultivate the patience of science. Let him linger—at any rate, let *me* linger—in the place of popular entertainment, whatever it may be; and take very careful note (if necessary in a notebook) of the way in which ordinary human beings do really talk about each other. As he is a scientific inquirer with a notebook, it is very likely that he never saw any ordinary human beings before. But if he will listen carefully, he will observe a certain tone taken toward friends, foes, and acquaintances; a tone which is, on the whole, creditably genial and considerate, though not without strong likes and dislikes. He will hear abundant, if sometimes bewildering, allusion to the well-known weaknesses of Old George; but many excuses also, and a certain generous pride in conceding that Old George is quite the gentleman when drunk; or that he told the policeman off proper. Some celebrated idiot, who is always spotting winners that never win, will be treated with almost tender derision; and, especially among the poorest, there will be a true Christian pathos in the reference to those who have been "in trouble" for habits like burglary and petty larceny. And as all these queer types are called up like ghosts by the incantation of gossip, the inquirer will gradually form the impression that there is one kind of man, probably only one kind of man, perhaps only one man, who is really disliked. The voices take on quite a different tone in speaking of him; there is a hardening and solidification of disapproval and a new coldness in the air. And this will be all the more curious because, by the current modern theories of social or anti-social action, it will not be at all easy to say why he should be such a monster or what exactly is the matter with him. It will be hinted at only in singular figures of speech, about a gentleman who is mistakenly convinced that he owns the street; or sometimes that he owns the earth. Then one of the social critics will say, " 'E comes in 'ere and 'e thinks 'e's Gawd Almighty." Then the scientific inquirer will shut his notebook with a snap and retire from the scene, possibly after paying for any drinks he may have consumed in the cause of social science. He has got what he wanted. He has been intellectually justified. The man in the pub has precisely repeated, word for word, the theological formula about Satan.

Pride is a poison so very poisonous that it not only poisons the virtues; it even poisons the other vices.

This is what is felt by the poor men in the public tavern when they tolerate the tippler or the tipster or even the thief, but feel something fiendishly wrong with the man who bears so close a resemblance to God Almighty. And we all do in fact know that the primary sin of pride has this curiously freezing and hardening effect upon the other sins. A man may be very susceptible and in sex matters rather loose; he may waste himself on passing and unworthy passions, to the hurt of his soul, and yet always retain something which makes friendship with his own sex at least possible and even faithful and satisfying. But once let that sort of man regard his own weakness as a strength, and you have somebody entirely different. You have the lady-killer, the most beastly of all possible bounders, the man whom his own sex almost always has the healthy instinct to hate and despise. A man may be naturally slothful and rather irresponsible, he may neglect many duties through carelessness, and his friends may still understand him so long as it is really a careless carelessness. But it is the devil and all when it becomes a careful carelessness. It is the devil and all when he becomes a deliberate and self-conscious Bohemian, sponging on principle, preying on society in the name of his own genius (or rather of his own belief in his own genius), taxing the world like a king on the plea that he is a poet, and despising better men than himself who work that he may waste. It is no metaphor to say that it is the devil and all. By the same fine old original religious formula, it is all of the devil. We could go through any number of social types illustrating the same spiritual truth. It would be easy to point out that even the miser, who is half ashamed of his madness, is a more human and sympathetic type than the millionaire who brags and boasts of his avarice, and calls it sanity and simplicity and the strenuous life. It would be easy to point out that even cowardice, as a mere collapse of the nerves, is better than cowardice as an ideal and theory of the intellect; and that a really imaginative person will have more sympathy with men who, like cattle, yield to what they know is panic, than with a certain particular type of prig who preaches something that he calls peace. Men hate priggishness because it is the dryest form of pride.

Thus there is a paradox in the whole position. The spiritual idea of the evil of pride, especially spiritual pride, was dismissed as a piece of mysticism not needed by modern morality, which is to be purely social and practical. And, as a fact, it is very specially needed because the morality is social and practical. On the assumption that we need care for nothing except making other human beings happy, this is quite certainly the thing that will make them unhappy. The practical case against pride, as a mere source of social discomfort and discord, is, if possible, even more self-evident than the more mystical case against it, as a setting up of the self against the soul of the world. And yet though we see this thing on every side in modern life, we really hear very little about it in modern literature and ethical theory. Indeed, a great deal of modern literature and ethics might be meant specially for the encouragement of spiritual pride. Scores of scribes and sages are busy writing about the importance of self-culture and self-realization; about how every child is to be taught to develop his personality (whatever that may be); about how every business man must devote himself to success, and every successful man must devote himself to developing a magnetic and compelling personality; about how every man may become a superman (by taking Our Correspondence Course) or, in the more sophisticated and artistic type of fiction, how one specially superior superman can learn to look down on the mere mob of ordinary supermen who form the population of that peculiar world. Modern theory, as a whole, is rather encouraging egoism. But we need not be alarmed about that. Modern practice, being exactly like ancient practice, is still heartily discouraging it. The man with the strong magnetic personality is still the man whom those who know him best desire most warmly to kick out of the club. The man in a really acute stage of self-realization is a no more pleasing object in the club than in the pub. Even the most enlightened and scientific sort of club can see through the superman, and see that he has become a bore. It is in practice that the philosophy of pride breaks down; by the test of the moral instincts of men wherever two or three are gathered together; and it is the mere experience of modern humanity that answers the modern heresy.

There is indeed another practical experience, known to us all, even more pungent and vivid than the actual unpopularity of the bully or the bumptious fool. We all know that there is a thing called egoism that is much deeper than egotism. Of all spiritual diseases it is the most intangible and the

[65]

most intolerable. It is said to be allied to hysteria; it sometimes looks as if it were allied to diabolic possession. It is that condition in which the victim does a thousand varying things from one unvarying motive of a devouring vanity; and sulks or smiles, slanders or praises, conspires and intrigues, or sits still and does nothing, all in one unsleeping vigilance over the social effect of one single person. It is amazing to me that in the modern world, that chatters perpetually about psychology and sociology, about the tyranny with which we are threatened by a few feeble-minded infants, about alcoholic poisoning and the treatment of neurotics, about half a hundred things that are near the subject and never on the spot—it is amazing that these moderns really have so very little to say about the cause and cure of a moral condition that poisons nearly every family and every circle of friends. There is hardly a practical psychologist who has anything to say about it that is half so illuminating as the literal exactitude of the old maxim of the priest: that pride is from hell. For there is something awfully vivid and appallingly fixed about this madness at its worst, that makes that short and antiquated word seem much more apt than any other. And then, as I say,

[66]

the learned go wandering away into discourses about drink or tobacco, about the wickedness of wine-glasses or the incredible character of public houses. The wickedest work in this world is symbolized not by a wine-glass, but by a looking-glass; and it is not done in public houses, but in the most private of all private houses which is a house of mirrors.

The phrase would probably be misunderstood; but I should begin my sermon by telling people not to enjoy themselves. I should tell them to enjoy dances and theaters and joy rides and champagne and oysters; to enjoy jazz and cocktails and night clubs if they can enjoy nothing better; to enjoy bigamy and burglary and any crime in the calendar, in preference to this other alternative; but never to learn to enjoy themselves. Human beings are happy so long as they retain the receptive power and the power of reaction in surprise and gratitude to something outside. So long as they have this they have, as the greatest minds have always declared, a something that is present in childhood and which can still preserve and invigorate manhood. The moment the self within is consciously felt as something superior to any of the gifts that can be brought to it, or any of the adventures that it may enjoy, there has appeared a sort of self-devouring fastidiousness and a disenchantment in advance, which fulfills all the Tartarean emblems of thirst and of despair.

Difficulties can easily be raised, of course, in any such debate by the accident of words being used in different senses; and sometimes in quite contrary senses. For instance, when we speak of somebody being "proud of" something, as of a man being proud of his wife, or a people proud of its heroes, we really mean something that is the very opposite of pride. For it implies that the man thinks that something outside himself is needed to give him great glory; and such a glory is really acknowledged as a gift. In the same way, the word will certainly be found misleading, if I say that the worst and most depressing element in the mixed elements of the present, and the immediate future, seems to me to be an element of impudence. For there is a kind of impudence that we all find either amusing or bracing, as in the impudence of the gutter-snipe. But there again the circumstances disarm the thing of its real evil. The quality commonly called "cheek" is not an assertion of superiority; but rather a bold attempt to balance inferiority. When you walk up to a very wealthy and powerful nobleman and play-

fully tip his hat over his eyes (as is your custom),
you are not suggesting that you yourself are above
all human follies, but rather that you are capable of
them, and that he also ought to have a wider and
richer experience of them. When you dig a royal
duke in the waistcoat, in your playful manner, you
are not taking yourself too seriously, but only, perhaps, not taking him so seriously as is usually
thought correct. This sort of impudence may be
open to criticism, as it is certainly subject to dangers.
But there is a sort of hard intellectual impudence
which really treats itself as intangible to retort or
judgment, and there are a certain number among the
new generations and social movements who fall into
this fundamental weakness. It is a weakness, for it
is simply settling down permanently to believe what
even the vain and foolish can only believe by fits
and starts, but what all men wish to believe and are
often found weak enough to believe—that they
themselves constitute the supreme standard of
things. Pride consists in a man making his personality the only test, instead of making the truth
the test. It is not pride to wish to do well, or even
to look well, according to a real test. It is pride to
think that a thing looks ill because it does not look

like something characteristic of oneself. Now in the general clouding of clear and abstract standards, there is a real tendency today for a young man (and even possibly a young woman) to fall back on that personal test simply for lack of any trustworthy impersonal test. No standard being sufficiently secure for the self to be moulded to suit it, all standards may be moulded to suit the self. But the self as a self is a very small thing and something very like an accident. Hence arises a new kind of narrowness, which exists especially in those who boast of breadth. The skeptic feels himself too large to measure life by the largest things, and ends by measuring it by the smallest thing of all. There is produced also a sort of subconscious ossification which hardens the mind not only against the traditions of the past, but even against the surprises of the future. *Nil admirari* becomes the motto of all nihilists; and it ends, in the most complete and exact sense, in nothing.

If I had only one sermon to preach, I certainly could not end it in honor without testifying to what is in my knowledge the salt and preservative of all these things. This is but one of a thousand things in which I have found the Catholic Church to be right when the whole world is perpetually tending

[70]

to be wrong; and without its witness, I believe that this secret, at once a sanity and a subtlety, would be almost entirely forgotten among men. I know that I for one had hardly heard of positive humility until I came within the range of Catholic influence; and even the things that I love most, such as liberty, and the island poetry of England, had in this matter lost the way, and were in a fog of self-deception. Indeed, there is no better example of the definition of pride than the definition of patriotism. It is the noblest of all natural affections exactly so long as it consists of saying, "May I be worthy of England!" It is the beginning of one of the blindest forms of Pharisaism when the patriot is content to say, "I am an Englishman!" And I cannot count it an accident that the patriot has generally seen the flag as a flame of vision, beyond and better than himself, in countries of the Catholic tradition, like France and Poland and Ireland, and has hardened into this heresy of admiring merely his own breed and bone and inherited type, and himself as a part of it, in the places most remote from that religion, whether in Berlin or in Belfast. In short, if I had only one sermon to preach, it would be one that would profoundly annoy the congregation by bringing to their attention the permanent challenge of the Church. If I had only one sermon to preach, I should feel specially confident that I should not be asked to preach another.

THERE CAME ONE RUNNING

by Dr. Henry Noble MacCracken

There Came One Running

By Dr. Henry Noble MacCracken

IN THE ruins of the city of Philadelphia, a Greek settlement east of the Jordan River that was once included in Decapolis, the "Ten Towns," a manuscript may have been found in the ruins of a Hellenistic mansion of some pretensions. Or it may not. The (as yet tentative) translation is appended. The beginning is apparently lost, the leaves being torn. It begins thus:

Often as I leave Philadelphia the delightful— with its shocking name, scarcely justified by its imperial association—and take my way along the banks of the river Yabbok, I feel myself akin to the first Greek colonists of old. They went west, to Massilia, Gades, and the new Miletus; and I came east, to this barbarous land of Syrian and Arab. A land of extremes it is, assuredly, Philadelphia, City of the Girl who Loved—and Wed—her Brother, with its Greek citizens, its Egyptian manners, or lack of manners, and its Roman laws; and through it plunging the wild torrent Yabbok, fierce and untamed stream of the mountains. A new country, and a prosperous one, also, considering how recently it was settled and the savage barbarians expelled for our politer comfort. A beautiful country, I confess, too, and not inferior to my native Corinth, with plenteous rains, good soil, and much husbandry and cattle, and pleasant groves of palm and olive.

Of the people I cannot say so much, although at times their strange ways and customs provoke me to much thought. Thus yesterday, as I was passing by the way, I was made aware of a teacher of Galilee with some companion, who walked, and talked as they walked, with evident pleasure. I was reminded of the Grecian custom, for we also, in groves or on the porches of temples or market-places, are wont to discuss new things of every sort. There is something in the very act of walking conducive to good conversation, whether it be the slow rhythm of the marching feet that gives good cadence to well-chosen words, and a fitting congruity of mind and thought, or whether, the blood being better disposed by motion in the whole body, and every part active, the

[76]

organism is in a more perfect disposition to serve its master, the mind, I know not; but I have ever favored the peripatetics.

So I came near, and greeted the Galileans, and was courteously entreated to join them. As we fell into talk of things new and old, there came one running. . . . He was a Greek, I think, for he was tall, and fair of skin, unmixed with the brown of the Arab or the swart blood of the Jordan dwellers of the valley. Assuredly he was not a Jew, although his garments were of the Jewish mode. He was young. That was my first impression. I am now past youth, myself, and therefore when I see such a one I see my own youth lost, and I think in a strange and yearning way. Moreover, I am Greek, and to me youth is the most beautiful thing in the world, and a manly youth such as this most of all, in the full flush of vigor and strength, in pride and willfulness of health and activity. This is the God in man, valiancy and intelligence such as Socrates loved in Alcibiades. For what men love in youth is promise and expectation of what is to be fulfilled. Everyone who grows old ceases to change, and only receives an intensifying of his youthful genius. An old man, says Plato, can no more learn than he can run.

And something more in the youth also there was —eager desire, a zest of motion, and thrust of limb— that bespoke impetuosity and headlong energy. He had run, I think, far, for he was heated and be-dewed, and his tunic was overlaid with dust. He panted somewhat, too, and seemed under physical strain as though he were not perfectly in training for such a race. But though his body were in toil, his mind was more so. For his eyes glowed, and an eager light came forth from them, such as gleams from the young soldiers marching to their first battle, or the lover on his way to the tryst, or the merchant to his gains. There was will, strong and determined, relentless and confident, as of one accustomed to having his own way in the world. And I knew that he desired something mightily, and for this had run so swiftly to overtake this teacher.

And suddenly, ere I was aware of his intention (for I was not of the nearest in the group to see, being mindful not to mix too closely with the peasant Galileans in the teacher's party), suddenly I per-ceived that he had kneeled at the wanderer's feet and, all in a gasp of quick-drawn breath, had poured

[78]

forth his petition. Not then did I learn what it
was, but I was intrigued none the less. What a picture it made, fit to be painted on a vase of red and
black by Callimachus or Charmides. The calm scene
of the evening sunset time, the quiet wayside, broken
only by the water falling over rocks; the little group
of wanderers, staffs in hand, following this grave
and quiet man as he talked; and then the sudden
irruption of youth, tempestuous and hardy, questioning and exorbitant of attention, usurping the
thought of all in his swift demand. Such a scene,
I thought, might once have inspired one of the best
of the immortal dialogues, were there any Platos to
be found nowadays.

The young suppliant had asked a question, vital to
him, no doubt, since he came to ask it of such a one.
He was rich, anyone might see—there is money to
be made in these parts—and he could buy easily all
the learning of the philosophers. Moreover, there
were educated men in the town, men filled, like myself, with ancient learning, who could have resolved
any knotty question of speech, any tangled skein of
the Law, any rule of the Roman governor, and almost for the asking. None of these would satisfy
him. Only one could give him the relief he sought.

[79]

That was clear, I saw, and I refrained from inter-
ruption, for when a disciple has chosen a master, one
were as good to try to catch a jackal in the way as to
divert him from his devotion. Man does not so
much wish to know, to learn, as to be like some one.
Therefore companionship of the worthy is your only
schooling worth having. Youth is full of strange
paradoxes, but none more strange than this, that although in youth the mind is free and dainty, resisting
compulsion (and most justly, for knowledge imposed by compulsion has no hold upon the mind),
yet youth of all ages cares most for the good opinion
of others, especially of him whose mind it reverences.

It was a great question, I was sure, by the intensity
of its asking. The answer would do something, it
was evident. Perhaps, like the answer to the Sphinx,
a kingship hung upon it; something of importance,
not only to this youth, but maybe to the world. The
ending of a journey, the completion of a great labor,
the philosopher's mystery, might be involved. A
world was perchance to be reformed, wrongs righted,
ruins made strong. Never had such a question been
asked before. It was elemental; upon the reply
hinged the destiny of his whole being. The moment
became suddenly pivotal to us; we felt ourselves at

the center of things, with the world looking on. The age clustered about the moment, as sometimes happens in the lives of men. When such occasions come, they say, one's whole course of action is determined. The past is explained and the future revealed, stretching away clear and distinct as a landscape after rain. If you know the time when it comes, you will be captain of your destiny and pilot of your way. If the moment passes and you are blind to it, it will not come again.

Something of all this was in my mind as I looked at the youth; something of it was but a reflection of his own steady and burning gaze, fixed on this man whose word he trusted. He wanted an answer, and upon the moment. It was crucial for him. The parting of the ways had been reached. Childhood was gone and manhood had come upon him. The commencement of authority and independence, the obligations of citizenship and rule, the responsibilities of wealth and place, weighed upon him, I was sure. They troubled him and irked his impatient spirit. But there was something more in this youth, beyond the mere externals of existence in a busy city. It was not the daily duties that cost him all this care. It was the mind that sought healing.

There were deeps within him that he knew not of, save now and then as passion drove him to a blaze of anger, of envy, or of ambition. Then he stood aghast and wondered at himself, and asked, "Was it I who did this, or another?" There arose at times the hungry and unsatisfied passion of love, ever growing by what it feeds on, and not finding what it sought. And he, high-minded and clean-hearted, started back appalled at the sight of himself as the mean slave of ignoble desire. The riddle to which he had asked an answer was just himself. And the answer must make him master of this undaunted steed, this wild Pegasus of will. He must have victory over his own spirit. For there are few youths who are at the same time quick, courageous, and gentle in self-control. Those who are quick to learn have also quick and ungovernable tempers. The slower and steadier are also more stupid and incapable of remembering. Happy he who in youth moves smoothly and successfully over the sea of knowledge to his appointed port, noiselessly and without storm, as on a river of oil.

This I knew by insight and was assured of it when I heard his angry rejoinder to the teacher's reply. That I had not caught, either, exactly; it was something ordinary, to this effect, "You know the answer as well as I; tell me."

So the youth rattled off his angry words; they were the commonplaces of the Law. Be good, true, obedient, kind. A dull and commonplace code it is indeed; nothing said of the intelligence, of the sense of beauty, of the experience of happiness, in all of it. Had he asked me, I might have made known to him the infinite power of man by his divine reason, the marvelous sensations of the mind and feeling attuned to perfect harmony, the ineffable pleasures of philosophy. But he did not ask me.

The teacher said to him, "That is right; that is the right answer," or words to that effect. What a dash to his hot spirits. What a chain to his proud feet, spurning the ground to be off for a flight through the empyrean! What! The vital moment at hand, the choice of all one's days to be made, the fork in the road reached, and just a friendly word of cheer, "Keep on; you're on the right track."

Thus the youth was grieved, though it was clear he reverenced his teacher, and he cried, "All this is old; I've done it ever since I was born. Am I to go to school all my life?"

I approved his indignation. It was well justified.

Is not there something more than mere piety to be performed here in these brief days that compose the span of life? To be a good son, husband, brother, father, a righteous ruler, an obedient servant of the Emperor of Rome, to pay one's taxes, whip the thieving slaves, plant the seed and reap the corn, is this all of life? Was our mind given us for this only? Is beauty on earth for this only? Is the strength and vigor of youth to waste itself in a stiff treading of the daily round like slaves on water wheels? Was not youth made to run? And it seemed to me that the youth was made for nothing else but thus to come running, and drop so gracefully upon his knees, and desire so earnestly the best thing he could ask. To inquire, to seek the mystery of earth and heaven—for this were we made. But such an answer would have done him no good, though it were true. It did not end desire.

He was tired of getting his duty by rote, and acting his rôle in the play of life. It seemed unreal and false to him. Everything was cut and dried, every step predicted a thousand years before. For every situation a hundred proverbs had been coined. Did he wish to spring across yonder ravine? Memory said, "Look before you leap." Did he hesitate in a choice of action? Memory whispered, "He who hesitates is lost." Everything provided, even in neat opposites, a pair in a bundle, made up and packed in the market, ready for use. Experience was a packet of figs, dried and pressed and covered. He was tired of it. There must be some other way.

Well, there was, it seemed. For as he gave vent to his youthful resentment, the teacher spoke. Then I realized, then only, I stood beside a master. His gaze enkindled the lad, his voice came strong and appealing, his form took on sternness and courage, resolution incarnate, greater than Pompey when he rode this way years ago. "Very well," he said, as I recall it; "give everything away and come."

It was like a trumpet calling the troops into action. It sounded like the words of a general to his best-trained men. It honored the youth with consideration of his potential worth. He was chosen. He might then choose. He was free.

This was what he wanted; had wanted all along. Yet he did not come. Confronted with the imperative, he flinched. He turned pale, looked at the teacher once imploringly, and, seeing only the summons, he rose and turned and went his way, and we saw him no more.

Born to command, he could not be commanded. He could not brook the idea that it took more courage to obey than to rule; that the soldier in the ranks is really bravest of the brave.

Born to enjoy, he could not visualize himself far out in the desert somewhere, away from cities and highways, alone with mountain tops and lonely gardens. He had seen the world in terms of conquest, not of conquering. The completed act, not the action, allured him. He would be a learned man, without ever being a man of learning, much less a learning man. Beside him from day to day stalked a shadow of fear that never left him; born of what inner experience who may say? Whatever it had been, it was now covered over with the rich gild of possession, known of none. And suddenly, in the crisis, it sprang up and conquered the citadel of his soul.

He had had two choices offered him, like Hercules or King Solomon, of whom the Jews tell their fables. Either he might live the daily life of men, taking things as they came day by day, doing his best by his lights, living up to the highest he knew, erring and stumbling in the dark at times, but keeping on with the task of life with simple courage. Living so, he would daily learn and grow in proportion as he applied the knowledge that he had. His would be a learning life, growing wise as the years passed. Such are the lives of most good persons. As time goes on, and they advance in years, and come more into contact with realities, they learn by experience to see and feel the truth of things. Thus they come to change many of their opinions, and the great appears small to them, and the easy difficult, speculations being overturned by the facts of life, as a light chariot by a broken stone in the pavement of the road.

Or he might greatly dare. He might all at once cut the encumbering threads of mere subsistence, and give himself wholly to truth. For this he must be himself of superior fiber. He must have the physical strength, the mental vigor, the resolute courage, the steadfast will. He must forego much, be willing to forego all. Socrates saw the cup of hemlock, but he did not falter. Such a summons was the youth's, and he could not measure up to it. I do not blame him. There are few who accept in its full implication the life of learning. But when they do, the world moves on a little faster upon its center.

His was a great opportunity, I could not help

reflecting. This Decapolis is a wonderful new country, thinly settled as yet, but fertile, and with a vig-
orous, intelligent population. Much is yet to be
done in the way of highways and irrigation. The
savage nations to the east and south must be subjugated and brought under our sway, enlightened
yet firm, the benefits of which they will themselves
eventually acknowledge when admitted to the citizenship of Rome and the culture of Greece. And
for this task we need youth, strong and brave, ruthless and determined, disciplined and sound on all
points of faith and practice. Worship the emperor,
obey the prefect, stand by the eagle, follow the fasces
where they go. Of what use are all these questions
and doubts? Clear as the Syrian sky is the destiny
of this favored land, preferred of all the gods.
Decapolis needs leadership. It was his, almost for
the asking.

Yet he went away, crushed and broken by the very
greatness of his opportunity. He desired that greatness. Only he could not see it in its daily terms, or
in the concentrated meaning of a vital moment. He
saw his career as an end in itself, and loved it too
dearly either to share it with his fellows, or to risk
all on a great venture.

It was sad to observe. It was the tragedy, I thought, of youth. The lad was broken on the wheel of circumstance. Was it his fault that in this town, in this year of the emperor, no easy way to success was evident? The waste of such a life struck to my heart. And as I looked at the Galilean, I could feel his own sadness also. There were love and heartbreak in his eyes. He did not blame him, I could see. It was circumstance. He was unfitted for the choice thrust on him by his very opportunities of wealth and power.

Fate, or circumstance, call it what you will, is always unjust to youth. Human nature bids us cry out in agony when the innocent and young are thus sacrificed. Iphigenia, sacrificed to promote the sailing of the fleet; Antigone, slain because she loved her brother; Cassandra, wise and helpless waif of destiny—such figures fill me with pity and with fear. But they are figures of legend, myths of long ago. Here, under my very eyes, I saw a similar tragedy wrought out in terms of human loss and wreckage.

I wanted to hurry after the youth, to bid him be of good courage. He must not take it so hard. Another chance would come his way. Some other teacher might give him a more pleasing answer.

Maybe war would come, and his fair chance to be a general. Perhaps Herod would hear of his good government and promote him. Anyway, what difference did it make that a Galilean had for a moment laid bare his secret fear? None else knew, indeed the whole countryside must praise him for a prominent young man.

These and other words of hollow comfort rose all too easily to my mind. But in vain. The young man was gone and I should have had to run to catch up with him. It was, besides, not my affair. What was to be would be. Two words of mine would not avert necessity, and I was more interested, after all, in the teacher than in the taught.

So I went up to the Galilean and said, "Master, what was the boon he asked of thee?" And he replied, "Life." And he went on with his friends and departed.

Life? That brave youth, endowed with courage, beauty, and skill, asking this outlander for "life"? Will youth never learn? Has it not youth? What does it want else, in the name of Apollo? Why should it fret over knowledge, or justice, or righteousness, or fame, or honor? These are shadows;

youth itself is the only substance. So says my Epi-
curus, wisest of men. For youth is joy and freedom.

And yet, as I write, I cannot put out of my mind
the eager form of the one who came running and
knelt at the teacher's feet, and with questioning gaze
asked for the gift of Life. Perhaps, after all, youth
needs one thing more to be perfect.

HOW TO BECOME A CHRISTIAN
by Lord Hugh Cecil

How to Become a Christian

By Lord Hugh Cecil

THE question is seldom asked, "What really makes us Christians?" We see and know all sorts of degrees of faith and unbelief. Some people are Christians without doubt, some have been Christians but have lost their faith; some have not lost their faith but feel it to be in certain respects precarious; some mean on a future day to look more closely into the matter; others, caring but little, drift along without anxiety, uncertain and indefinite;—in short there are all sorts of degrees of orthodoxy or unbelief or doubt or vagueness, made practically tolerable because the unbeliever or doubter still clings to the main consequences of religious belief in respect to morality. But how do all these people get where they are?

A man accepts the Christian faith either from training in childhood or by conversion when he is grown up. Nearly everyone in our country who holds the Christian faith, holds it because he was so taught as a child. Sometimes there is no disturbance of this religious faith; sometimes the experiences of life, new currents of opinion, and, it may be feared, moral faults and deficiencies, beat against religious faith and shake it and wholly or partly overthrow it. For some men there has been an attack in the mind on faith, and it has been repelled, it may be at once or after a time. The man who goes through such an experience will usually persuade himself that his opinion has been ultimately determined by a process of reasoning; but acute observers often find that the reasoning processes of the mind are in fact themselves determined by inclinations or prejudices of which the mind may be totally unconscious or only half aware, but which, in fact, decide the conclusion to which reason comes. Here is found the power of any moral inconsistency with Christian teaching, and here also the very strong influence of what may be called intellectual fashion, a sense of the congruity of an opinion with the general system of thought which prevails. We do not reject belief in fairies because we have carefully investigated the question of their reality, but because that sort of belief is incongruous with our general

[96]

habits of thought. This may be a safe way of deciding, but is not always so. A great many people, for example, rejected mesmerism, as it was called, because it sounded like an hysterical imposture. But they were in this mistaken, and, under the name of hypnotism, mesmerism has come to be recognized as a real experience and part of the physical system. At any rate, whatever may determine the decision of the mind about religious faith, the sequence of experience is that the child receives and accepts Christianity on the authority of his teachers, that if he does not retain belief unshaken it is because of a hostile influence of one kind or another which occasions disturbance of mind and leaves him altogether without faith or with faith in some degree shaken or upset.

Let us here ask a further question, with which we might have begun, What is the Christian religion? Or a still more rudimentary question, What is religion? This question seems to me to be often answered amiss. The word connotes a bond and means essentially (I suggest) a personal relation with the unseen. The relation may be a reality or a delusion. Religion, as we speak, may be true or false, but its essence is in this relation through the veil that hides from us the invisible world. And Christianity purports to be a relation with a person, with a personal God. God has, as Christians believe, revealed Himself to man in some degree through nature, in a greater degree by a progressive revelation to the Jewish people, culminating in the incarnation of God Himself as a man in the person of Jesus of Nazareth. And it is through Christ that we enter into relation with God. Moreover, we are taught to believe that it is by the power of God that we are enabled to enter into this relation. God is thus manifested to us after a threefold mode: He is the ultimate object of our devotion; He is the Saviour and Redeemer by Whom we, in spite of our sins, can obtain access to His divine nature; He is the Spirit Who, from within us, shapes our purpose and faith and leads us to be saved by Him, the Saviour, and to adoration of and union with His perfect divinity. This relation is not merely individual; it is essentially social: the Divine Spirit incorporates the individual in a society of which the Head is Christ and in the corporate life of which man draws near to God. All this expresses a mystical experience; by "mystical" I mean an experience which is partly and only partly intellectually intelligible. A mystery may be defined as a half-disclosed truth, like a mountain with its summit in the clouds. And the Christian religion is such a mystery. The mystical relation of the worshiper to God is a perfectly real experience, though it is not an experience of which a complete intellectual description can be given. But though the intellect cannot describe the experience, it can partly explain and justify it. The personal relation which constitutes religion is sustained by a certain body of theological opinion expressed in our creeds. The doctrines of the Trinity and of the Incarnation can be stated; and though the statements are avowedly incomplete and must be put in a form which presents a contradiction or at the least an inconsistency, and are therefore incapable of complete rational assimilation, yet they make paths down which we can spiritually move and achieve the experience which is the essence of our religion; that is, we can enter into this relation with God after the fashion that our theological rules direct us. Theology regulates religion and justifies it against the imputation of being a mere imaginative delusion; but theology is not itself religion. Theology is a function of the intellect. Like other sciences, it is pursued with most success by the most able

[99]

minds, and skill in it is attained by study and learning. But religion is experienced without elaborate
study or learning or more instruction than is needed
to be able to enter upon a relation with the unseen.
The relation is the reality; theology is only the explanation of it. For example, a person is overcome
with a deep and depressing sense of his own sin-
fulness. By prayer and confession to God he receives
a sense of forgiveness, redemption, and salvation.
The whole experience seems to him of indisputable
reality, and it does in fact change both his happiness
and his conduct. He is, however, not necessarily
able to expound a word of the theology which re-
lates to his experience. The theologian will tell him
about the Incarnation and the Atonement and how
sin is destroyed by the righteousness of Christ. This
explanation will give the converted penitent confidence and stability. He will feel the more sure that
he has not been the dupe of emotion or fancy which
has misled him to mistake delusion for truth. But
while theology thus shelters and rationalizes the actual experience, it is the experience itself that constitutes religion and is the true bond which connects
the individual with God. And if theology is not
the same thing as religion, neither is morality. The

[100]

penitent who has turned from his sins and been converted, who has been instructed that his sins have
been atoned for and that he is redeemed, goes forward to a life regulated by moral rules and sustained
in whatever lapses by a settled purpose to strive toward the righteousness of God. This new moral
life is the consequence of religion; it is at every
point sustained by a persistence in religious practice
and the enjoyment of religious experience; but the
moral conduct thus achieved and strengthened only
manifests religion and depends upon it; it is not
religion itself.

It is important to insist upon the truth that religion
is a personal relation to God, and the Christian religion a personal relation through Christ to God,
because other ways of defining it have led to confusion and, it may be feared, to a good deal of
unreality among those who have been brought up
to be religious, but have never really understood
what religion means. Writers who have either lost
belief in Christianity altogether or accept only
vaguely and in part the full creed of Christendom,
often seem unaware of what religion really is and
how to seek it. And the whole process of apologetic
controversy becomes confused because the dispu-

tants begin, so to speak, at the wrong place. They do not start with the relation and expound it, and then discuss whether it is most likely to be a real relation or a delusion of the imagination, and go on to arrange the whole body of Christian apologetics by way of support to the proposition that the experienced relation is a reality and not a dream; they begin, on the contrary, by arguing this or that part of Christian theology as though it were a proposition to be proved, and if proved, to be accepted, and that religion would somehow or another spring out of that intellectual acceptance. But this way of presenting the matter is not the way in which the human mind does, as a matter of fact, commonly become religious. The most that such a way of proceeding can really do is to make a man try after religion, and it very seldom achieves even this. A great sorrow, a vivid sense of the difference between good and evil, and of the appalling power of sin —these things are much more potent to make people try and find religion by actually entering into the religious relation than any intellectual argument. Even mere assertion, if it be obviously sincere and confident, does much more to induce the doubting to make trial of the religious relation than a process of reasoning. And those, again, who are satisfied with a certain standard of godly conduct and suppose that that is all that matters in the religious life, are the enemies of their own happiness. It may well be that such lives, when they are thoroughly lived, are sufficient to make a person have that desire for approach to God which is, I suppose, the essence of salvation. But a merely moral life is certainly not sustained by the comfort, peace, and joy of the true religious relation. Those who are satisfied with what they call a straight and honest life do, in fact, walk in desert places, and, whatever mercies they may hereafter receive from God, do not now know the quenching of the inward thirst which man has for God. They may be righteous, but they are not happy.

If, then, it be admitted that religion is in itself neither opinion nor conduct, but a mystical relation with an unseen presence, the all-important question follows: Is this relation a fanciful delusion, having no existence outside the mind of the person who believes in it, or is it a true access to the unseen world, to the person of the external Creator, Saviour, and Sanctifier? Is the Christian religion true or fanciful? Those who would give the answer that it is the work of fancy hardly seem to feel how difficult their answer is. For it is the undisputed fact that people have for nineteen hundred years past entered into this relation, which we call the Christian Religion, and believed in it, and have acted upon it, and been transformed in character by it, and have made sacrifices and efforts in response to it as though it were real. All sorts of people have done this, of all sorts of temperaments, and they have done it alike in primitive and mediæval and modern times, notwithstanding the immense revolutions in mental outlook that have taken place. The Renaissance has come and the Reformation and the Democratic Movement and the Humanitarian Movement and Rationalism, and all the discoveries of science; and yet, though Christian people have in some respects modified their theological opinions, the essence of their religion remains unchanged. They still worship as Christians, still feel that they know Jesus Christ as a living person, still confess sins, still believe themselves to be redeemed and forgiven, still feel that by the power of the Spirit they are led nearer to Christ, still make that approach by the ordinances of the Church, still receive Holy Communion and are sustained and uplifted by it; and

[104]

they who do these things still include persons of all sorts of temperaments, and among them sober, unimaginative, and learned men, as well as others of a more emotional and enthusiastic type. Christianity is not in the least dead; it is, on the contrary, vigorously alive, strongly influencing human action, of vast importance in the inner life of countless multitudes. If all this spring out of fancy and delusion, how surprisingly strong and how surprisingly valuable is the influence of fancy and delusion. The world has been transformed by it. By common agreement it has been the strongest of all the influences at work since Christ preached and died. If the stories of His nativity and His resurrection and all the miracles of His ministry, of that Ascension by which He passed out of this world, and of the coming of the Divine Spirit Who came to bring Him and His disciples forever together, united as Head and body, till the end of time—if all this be folk-lore and legend, how highly must we value folk-lore and legend. Men, it seems, would be poor and miserable without their delusions. Except for the capacity of mankind to believe falsehood, all that is best in our civilization would not have existed.

I find this a very incredible position; yet it seems

forced on those who deny the truth of Christianity. I suppose they would rejoin that much of what I have said about Christianity might equally be said about Mohammedanism; yet no one thinks Mohammedanism true. To that I should rejoin that in so far as Mohammedanism is concerned with elementary fundamentals—that there is a God and that it is possible to be in relation with Him—it does indeed speak the truth. All religions, Christian and non-Christian, are so far in agreement: they claim that there is an unseen world and that it is possible to have relation with it. And I should press my opponent to admit that you must either say that all mankind are under delusion or that at least it is true that there is a God and that you can have relation with Him. But further, a fair view of Christianity and Mohammedanism and of their influence on the world confirms what Christianity says of Mohammedanism, but not what Mohammedanism says of Christianity. Mohammedanism teaches that Christianity is insufficient, faithless, and degraded: Christianity allows to Mohammedanism only very rudimentary truth crusted over with absurd errors and hateful wickedness. The verdict of experience is for Christianity; it is among Christianized mankind that what we call civilization has come into be-ing and made progress; and it is found that Christianity is possible to the most highly civilized men, while Mohammedanism is not. Mohammedan-ism, though its first impact on paganism seems wholesome, cannot go far; what is good in its life seems to dry up, and what remains is pestilent rather than healthy to mankind. If there be a God, and if He has revealed Himself to men—a little to Mo-hammedans and far more perfectly to Christians— this is exactly what we should expect. The more perfect revelation carried men further than that which only contains a little truth, corrupted and pol-luted by much evil. The main conclusion of a sur-vey of the phenomena of religious belief remains unshaken; that if you reject Christianity as untrue, you must first attribute to delusion a degree of power which is both surprising and alarming, and secondly, you must recognize that this power of delusion is most beneficent. Yet this is against one of our most confident moral intuitions: we are so made that we cannot believe that falsehood is a good thing and has a good influence in the world.

One may carry this appeal to experience further in another way. According to the Christian faith,

God, having made men and the world, revealed Himself to them through the Jewish race and ultimately, in the person of Jesus, He became man. If this happened, clearly it would be the greatest event in human history; and precisely the coming of Christ is the greatest event in human history. If the incarnation of God happened, it would be the turning-point on which everything else would depend; and precisely the life and death of Christ is the turning-point on which everything else depends. On the negative hypothesis, the greatest event in history, the turning-point on which everything else depends, is the appearance of a remarkable peasant Jew, with an unusual talent for epigram and parable, who taught sublime morality and was persecuted by the Jewish priesthood and unjustly put to death by the Roman governor—surely a surprisingly commonplace series of events to be the greatest thing in human history. Christian theology fits into history like a wanted piece into a dissected puzzle. The Christian hypothesis makes it possible to tell the story of human history naturally and without strain. If we believe in a God Who made men, it is certainly natural to believe that He wished to save and sanctify them. Only, indeed, by some such belief are

[108]

we able to satisfy our instinct that God is good, in face of the terrible experience of the evils of creation. The goodness of God becomes credible if He Himself, the Creator, has come down to suffer with His creatures, and to endure that wicked men should treat Him as Christ was treated and should die as Christ died. And that perfect goodness should be so rejected and persecuted is what our knowledge of human nature would lead us to expect. That the incarnate God and perfect Man should be hated and cruelly killed by wicked men is most natural. That He should not be forever conquered by their wickedness, but should ultimately triumph over them, is what the believer in righteous omnipotence would expect; and the whole course of history from the Crucifixion downward witnesses to and agrees with this expectation. "If Christ be not raised then is your faith vain and ye are yet in your sins" is, in all its implications, a strong argument. That vast structure, the conversion of mankind to be Christian, rests on the resurrection of Christ. Is it credible that so great a thing can really rest on fiction?

These considerations appear to me to create a strong, reasonable presumption in favor of the truth of Christianity. And it will be observed that the actual evidence for the reality of the Christian revelation has not yet been brought into consideration at all. What Christianity has done, what it is still doing, its effect upon the world and upon history, are indisputable; and the hearing of the evidence of its truth begins under the influence of the presumption that what has produced so far-reaching and wholesome an effect upon mankind and is still felt to be a reality by vast numbers of human beings, and by some of the wisest among them, cannot rest on delusion.

I do not propose to pursue the path of apologetics any further; there are plenty of books about Christian evidences accessible to anyone interested. Indeed, the purpose of this paper is more narrow. It is to remind readers that religion is neither a series of propositions to be accepted by the intellect nor a series of rules of conduct to be observed, but essentially a real but mystical—that is a half-understood—relation to an unseen Person. It follows that religion is a thing to be entered upon, to be achieved, to be realized, to be practiced, to be enjoyed, rather than merely to be believed in—though of course belief is necessary. If a person desires to become a

Christian, being satisfied, for example, that Christians are happier than he is, the way to do it is to attempt to become initiated into the relation with the unseen; and this is done, first, by a certain moral preparation. For though moral inconsistencies are not fatal to the religious experience if they are not deliberately acquiesced in, yet for anyone deliberately and consistently to follow a way of life he believes to be irreconcilable with a religious relation to Christ is fatal to the realization of that relation. What is required is the adoption of a high and rigorous standard of Christian morals, notwithstanding any lapses through weakness. This standard must comprise the absolute rejection of all hatred, malice, and uncharitableness—which is the most mortal of spiritual poisons—and all unchastity and the unreserved acceptance of unselfishness as the rule of life to the degree that all mere self-assertion should be adjured. Given this moral preparation, anyone may say prayer, and prayer should express and support the moral standard of life; it should include prayer for grace and enlightenment and for a blessing on any person who might naturally be an object of hatred and resentment. Above all, the Lord's Prayer should be used. I suggest that as time goes

[111]

on the sense of a real personal relation with Christ will grow up and the seeker after religion will have achieved the first stage. He will be a Christian. About subsequent stages Christians are not agreed; but as I believe, the Christian religion is sacramental, and the relation with Christ is most deeply and completely realized by the offering and communion of the eucharist. If, then, the question is asked, "How can I be a Christian?" it is thus that it may be answered.

But if a person, though anxious to be a Christian, is unwilling to become one so long as he feels intellectual difficulties or objections, or as long as his intellect cannot give assent to what is implied by the practice of religion, then such a person should advert to the considerations I have pointed out, which create a presumption of truth in favor of Christianity, and, having weighed that presumption, should proceed to study the evidence for and against the truth of the Christian revelation and any particular question which seems to him important. It is quite right to do this if a man feels that loyalty to truth requires it. But it is well to remember all the time that it is not the way to become a Christian, but simply a preliminary required in order that afterward the way may be sought and pursued. The investigation of truth may be a duty, but it is not entering upon the religious relation. Sometimes the two processes may go on side by side: a man may try to be initiated into Christianity at the same time that he is studying Christian evidences. This is not amiss, supposing he always keeps it clear in his head that the studying of Christian evidences is what he owes to his loyalty to truth and is not in itself part of the practice of religion.

Nevertheless, loyalty to truth is most precious. Even at the outset of the religious relation the resolve to test truth is needed to save mysticism from developing into extravagance or superstition. And throughout the development of the relation the danger of superstition is always present and the discipline of an exact inquiry into truth is therefore never superfluous. The sense of obedience to the rational faculties which try and approve truth guards the mind from the inebriation of mystical experience and obliges it to hold itself in check, loyal to a standard external to itself which is recognized to be true. Truth arrived at by research disciplines religion; so, too, does the orthodoxy of theological formulas, respected because of the authority which

[113]

has framed them. Orthodoxy, like the candid investigation of truth, is a restraint on the emotions and fancies which easily mingle with the real religious experience. But, chastened by this discipline of truth, the essence of religion does lie in the relation to an unseen person and it is there to be sought.

Christianity is thus a thing to be experienced and practiced; it is a certain relation to be entered upon, and the function of inquiry and reason is to guard the religious experience from the danger of delusion and to discipline it into a strict faithfulness to truth.

FOR ALL BISHOPS AND OTHER
CLERGY

by Sheila Kaye-Smith

For All Bishops and Other Clergy

By Sheila Kaye-Smith

IF I had only one sermon to preach perhaps I might well take as my subject the failure of modern preaching. It would be interesting to look into the causes that have debased a noble art and fruitful religious exercise to the level of an edifying chat. The sermon, it seems to me, has a double function —to instruct the mind and to stir the emotions; but the modern sermon is a mere tickling of the ears. One sometimes finds it hard to realize that Christianity was first spread by sermons—that Paul of Tarsus and other early adventurers, by teaching and exhortation converted souls to Christ with little or no help from the written word. The Gospel is some scores of years older than the New Testament, and the men who carried that Gospel must have been very different preachers from the preachers of today. They must have preached with authority, with a single heart, a united experience, and a total dis-

[117]

regard of the judgments and standards of the world through which they moved with such romantic boldness.

In the Middle Ages the sermon was still honorable. The man in the street could not read, and depended on the spoken word for his education. Preaching was then a privilege and sometimes an adventure—the delivering or the hearing of a sermon might involve a considerable journey. A sermon which many of the congregation had come several miles to hear, and which would be their only intellectual sustenance for several weeks, required and received careful preparation, neither would it be undertaken by anyone who was not well fitted to the task.

When preaching became more general its quality deteriorated, and with the spread of education the need for it as a teaching medium grew less. In the eighteenth century sermon-reading became a popular religious pastime, though its popularity was not long-lived, as the sermon is above all a subjective and personal affair, that loses much of its force in print. The writing of sermons to be read instead of heard also had a disastrous effect upon the style, robbing it of spontaneity and leaving it a prey to the advancing tide of Johnsonian English which had already swamped more than half the literature of that day.

The aridity of the eighteenth-century sermon, whether preached or written, led naturally to such a reaction as the Evangelical Revival, which was above all a revival of preaching—though it is interesting to note that it also introduced the tract. It set forth the doctrines of Evangelical Christianity by means of the printed word, using the spoken word chiefly for the purpose of exciting the emotions. Men and women no longer listened to sermons in order to be taught lessons of faith and conduct, but in order to have their emotions stirred. The success of a preacher was judged by his power to produce emotional disturbances in his congregation. The preaching of Wesley was received with shouts, amens, and alleluias, or even with physical convulsions, and such phenomena still sometimes accompany preaching of a revivalistic type.

To instruct and to stimulate seem to me the two main functions of preaching. At different periods one or the other has predominated—perhaps sometimes unduly. But the sermon of today has apparently lost any reason it ever had for existing. It no longer instructs, it no longer stimulates either to terror or to ecstasy. And by a perverse development there can seldom have been more sermons preached than there are now. In fact, you might say that the greatness of the demand is one reason for the deterioration of the supply. In hundreds of churches and chapels throughout the land the wretched minister has to provide two discourses every Sunday. Only the stoutest oratorical and evangelical gifts could stand such a strain, and doubtless many a potential Donne or Wesley is annually staled and tired into something worse than silence.

When one comes to the successful preachers (I am, of course, speaking of this country only) one finds that, with certain exceptions, neither do they fulfill the main functions of preaching. They do not teach and they do not stir. Most of them seem to have for their model the newspaper leader, and deal with some moral, religious, or even social and political topic of the day, much as a newspaper leader of the better sort would deal with it. They do not speak with authority, but as the scribes. If, on the other hand, they lean to the emotional rather than to the intellectual side of things, all they produce is a mild edification, or that cowardly state of "feeling good" which is the enemy of true religion.

How one longs on one side for the clear spirit of Fenelon, for the piercing grace of Francis de Sales, for the light and sanity of Pascal; on the other for the fire of Savonarola, for the "enthusiasm" (I use the word in its eighteenth-century sense) of the Wesleys, or even of George Fox shouting, "Woe! Woe to the bloody city of Litchfield!" I know that there are preachers today who shout, "Woe!" but it is always from a safe distance. They will not shout Woe to Litchfield or any bloody city from its own market place.

The sermon today has lost its driving power, its inspiration; and it may have been helped toward this loss by the neglect and spoliation of its technique. It has become contracted and extinguished. These are leisureless times of haste, and every form of literary art has had to adapt itself to new conditions. In the case of the novel these have been beneficial. The cutting down of the length of the average novel to less than half of what it used to be has served to improve enormously the technique of novel-writing. The modern novel is all the better for losing curves and redundancies that were merely

[121]

dissipations of energy. But the sermon never expanded beyond the requirements of its art form. It had no outlying portions to lose; any amputations were vital. I have often been assured, and I can well believe it from my own experience of lecturing, that no technically good or intellectually satisfying sermon can be delivered in less than forty minutes. Who today will listen for half that time? The average length of the average sermon, generally tagged on to a service which has already exhausted the congregation's rather slender powers of attention, is, I suppose, about a quarter of an hour. In this time it is possible to do little more than give a sort of moral lecturette, a piece of topical commentary, an instruction on some small point. The only alternative is the devotional address, which is not suitable to all types of congregation.

As a step toward recovery I would venture to suggest that the sermon be no longer served as a common dish, but be set apart for special occasions. It is time we realized that notable pastoral gifts may not always be accompanied by the gift of eloquence. This is, of course, a definite drawback in denominations of which the services consist mainly of preaching. A minister who could not preach would have

comparatively few other ways of justifying his existence. But in the life of the average parish clergyman sermon-making does not bulk nearly so large.
To his congregation it may be the most important,
because the most interesting, part of the service, the
variable and personal part which it is their right and
their delight to criticize. But the modern priest,
especially in a town, knows that, apart from his
possession or lack of the power to make a good sermon, his other work gives him little opportunity for
doing so. His day is spent in a succession of duties
—the administration of sacraments, the reading of
offices, the visiting of the sick, the saving of sinners,
the instruction of inquirers, besides such study as is
only decent in a clerk in holy orders. . . . All day
long he is exercising the various functions of his
ministry, and yet upon him the whole time lies the
shadow of that sermon by which he shall principally
be judged. In five if not seven cases out of ten he
prepares insufficiently or not at all—especially if he
is aware, as many of the clergy are only too well
aware, that he has no special gifts in this direction,
and is wasting time that might be spent more profitably in other work.

The fact is that we need more specialization. We

need specialists among our clergy as among our doctors. We should not require them all to be general practitioners—or indeed Jacks-of-all-trades, since much of the modern cleric's work has nothing clerical about it. I would suggest something after the Continental plan, where a large staff of clergy often runs a large parish containing several churches. Sermons are delivered, perhaps only at the mother church, by those of the staff who really can preach. The others are not required to agonize themselves or their congregations by "taking their turn." One clergyman, perhaps, devotes himself chiefly to hearing confessions, another specializes in work among children, another who is musically gifted is appointed to sing the principal services. Each one does what he can do best, instead of attempting to do everything. The result is far greater efficiency in the various departments, and at the same time less man-power is required than when a single Jack-of-all-trades has isolated charge of a single church and parish.

I should like to have sermons preached in every town on the university plane—*i.e.,* a course delivered by some specially qualified preacher at a central church, apart from any service, and drawing a congregation from those who have already fulfilled their obligations of worship elsewhere. There could be a system of licensing and appointing preachers for this special work. As for the country districts, the time has long seemed ripe for the organization of a band of preaching friars, bringing the gifts of expert teaching and a much needed variety into rural parishes.

Of course it would be fatal to divorce the preaching and pastoral aspects of the ministry. Only a parish priest knows truly the special needs of his own people, and a lack of parochial experience would in many cases make the visiting preacher a curse rather than a blessing. But if we are to imagine the group-system of parishes existing and involving at least one expert preacher among the clergy, the visits of extra, licensed preachers would be something quite apart from the normal parish machinery, and this difficulty need not arise.

The parish clergy would still have in their hands the instruction of their people, and their deliverance from the burden of useless preaching would free them for a much-needed development of this work. It is astonishing how many priests in England take for granted that their congregations know at least the outlines of the Christian faith. They ignore almost entirely their opportunities for teaching, unless a few classes for confirmation candidates can be dignified by that name. Those who "enter" their church schools in the hours allowed for religious instruction often give lessons of the type satirized in that immortal work, *Huppim and Muppim and Ard.* As for the grown-ups it is taken for granted that they have no more to learn, and the Sunday sermon, which might be devoted to building on the foundations laid in youth—or perhaps in clearing them away and laying others more fitted to bear the weight of the superstructure—is given over to the enunciation of moral platitudes, or sometimes, when the preacher is very "enlightened," to a futile and superficial dealing with modern scientific, social, and political problems which would require an expert for their correct presentation, let alone solution.

The result is that people do not grow up religiously at all. However cultured and intelligent they may be in other ways, from a religious point of view they remain infantile. I would be ready to bet that there are thousands of adults who, if they use any prayers at all, still use the prayers they were taught at their mother's knee; and I have again and again met men and women whose minds in most matters are well informed, sane, imaginative, who can talk brilliantly on a variety of subjects, scientific, artistic, or political, who nevertheless, when they come to talk about religion, descend suddenly to the level of ignorant children. This is hardly surprising when one realizes that these people have had probably no religious instruction since their childhood's days, and are much in the same position as a would-be mathematician whose studies had been cut short in the third form.

Of course I know that religion is a life rather than a creed, but that increases rather than reduces the need for instruction. Practice is involved as well as theory, and is more difficult to learn. The life of a Christian requires as thorough and as specialized a training as the life of a scientist or an athlete. For by a Christian life I do not mean merely a moral life or even a humane and generous life—all these things have become instinctive with many citizens of a Christian country after nearly two thousand years of Christian civilization—but a life given over wholly to the practice of the presence of God. This and not mere personal or social morality should be the

[127]

ideal preached from every pulpit, though at the same time it should be acknowledged as an ideal, and not demanded as the normal performance of poor folk whose minds are full of every sort of religious inhibition. For them the Church should teach, as she provides, a compassionate minimum—knowing that nothing is at once more dangerous and more dull than "a religion for good people only." The tragedy of the modern pulpit in England is that as a rule it preaches just that sort of religion, with the additional outrage that the "goodness" involved is a purely natural goodness of personal and social behavior rather than the great adventure of grace.

Why are we so seldom taught anything of the life of prayer? "Prayer" for most people means only petition—asking God for things and hoping, but not expecting, we will get them. Who knows anything about the technique of prayer?—its development from vocal prayer to mental prayer, from mental prayer to the loving silence of the gazing soul? Who knows and who cares? And yet most of our modern difficulties about prayer are due to the fact that we persist in regarding it merely as petition. They would vanish if we were taught to see prayer as our conscious relationship with God, involving petition as conscious relationship with an earthly father will involve occasional requests, but involving far more of loving intercourse and silent companionship.

Why are we so seldom taught the history and philosophy of our religion? One reason, no doubt, is that history and philosophy are at a discount today, that biology and chemistry have taken their places in popular esteem. But biology and chemistry can never take the place of history and philosophy in any sound system of thought, and our unhistoric and un-philosophical scientists are as big a danger to modern thought as the unscientific historians and philos-ophers of an earlier day. Theology was called of old the "queen of sciences"—now the mere mention of it seems to make some people see red. It is even declared that Christ would have condemned theol-ogy—he who astounded the doctors of the rabbinical schools by his understanding and answers.

Our modern religion in this country is terribly, pathetically in need of theology—by which I mean that system of history and philosophy which alone can make reasonable our faith in God. I would not for one moment be thought to disparage the faith of those souls who have no need of reason—blessed are they! Every good Christian will join in his

Master's thanksgiving to the heavenly Father who has hid these things from the wise and prudent and revealed them unto babes. It is the revelation to the shepherds—running across a field to Bethlehem at the bidding of an angel.

But there were also the Wise Men who journeyed across a continent at the bidding of an astronomical calculation, and neither must we disparage them, though at the end of their effort and danger they found no more than the simple shepherds found. Besides, in these days there are special unwarrantable dangers for the simple-minded. We have thrown stumbling-blocks in the way to Bethlehem, and offended these little ones who believe. Our widespread, half-baked system of culture has worked havoc with hundreds of unsophisticated souls. The man in the street cannot open his newspaper and not read at least once a year, if not oftener, that the Christian faith has been severely shaken by some recent discovery. He believes it because, instead of theology, he has been taught to rely on the verbal inspiration of his Bible, or at least of his newspaper. He has never learned to read the New Testament as the young Church wrote it, and the Fathers read it, and he would probably be surprised at the

[130]

"modernism" of such theologians as St. Basil and St. Augustine.

Not long ago I saw in a daily newspaper a headline after this sort—"Scientist states possibility of spontaneous generation of life. What will Christianity do?" In an ensuing correspondence a well-known scientist held out over orthodox religion the threat that one day life will be manufactured in the chemist's laboratory. As a result, no doubt, many believers were hurt unprofitably, and many heretics rejoiced unwarrantably. In the only sermon I heard delivered on the subject the preacher roundly asserted that life was not autogenous, and never could be. And that was that.

And yet both St. Basil and St. Augustine believed in the spontaneous generation of life . . . they believed that life arose spontaneously through the action of the sun on the slime of river beds. They accepted it as a scientific dogma of their day, just as they accepted evolution. Later on, the Church accepted the revised verdict of science that life could not thus arise, but must come from already existing life. Nowadays, apparently, biology has once more changed its conclusions, and all sensible men are ready to accept them. All that some of them resent is being told that their acceptance involves a threat to the faith that through all these changes has stood unchanged.

If I had not one but a dozen sermons to preach I should preach on religion as a science and as an art. If the Christian religion is to hold its own in this modern scientific and artistic world we must cease to preach it as a haphazard agglomeration of facts and maxims, as legal morality or as subjective emotion. It is a science that has its hypotheses, and an art that has its technique. Of course it is also much more than this; I should venture to describe it as the sum total of all our human instincts and activities transfigured by communion with the person of Jesus Christ our Lord. But here again one is involved in clouds of misconception. To many of that vast multitude who have had no adult instruction the term "person" is blurred by images of human personality, and to many more of this same vast multitude Christ is little but a dim figure in the past. We see newspaper articles on "If Christ came to London," when only a little instruction in the living faith of Christians would do away with that "if." We hear the cry, "Back to the Carpenter,"

[132]

though I would challenge anyone to read the Gospels and see if they find a carpenter there.

We need instruction in the plain matters of faith if we are not to misconceive it, and consequently lose it when these misconceptions are attacked, as they quite rightly and generally are. As a step toward this I would plead for a total change in our modern system of preaching. Let us cease to give the name of "divine worship" to what has often been no more than a spiritual yawn. Not thus are obligations fulfilled and God's honor satisfied. For that we might profitably offer the treasures of dramatic beauty that are the inherited worship of Christendom. Let us regard the sermon rather as a part of our religious education, a sort of continuation class, a university extension lecture. And here I would plead for the delivery of sermons not only apart from the services, so that they need no longer be cramped by considerations of time and attention, but in circumstances where the congregation can ask questions and some sort of discussion can take place. This would be unthinkable under the usual conditions of preaching, but the inability to ask questions has often caused avoidable misunderstanding. I would also plead once more for the specialized preacher; for the shifting of the burden from the shoulders of wearied and worried parish ministers to those specially trained for the work. I would plead for sermons delivered not haphazard, but in orderly series, as many lectures are delivered now. There is still room for the soul-searching eloquence of Wesley's time, but it needs to be coupled with objective teaching or the results are likely to be merely subjective and emotional.

If I had only one sermon to preach it seems that the best I could do with it would be to entreat those who have, not one, but many sermons to preach, to make better use of their opportunities. There is no field in which ignorance is less blissful than the field of religion. Ignorance inevitably means loss. I have been impressed by the fact that every attack on Christianity that I have been able personally to examine has been based on a misconception. Clear teaching would have made it abortive and unnecessary. If only our teachers would abandon the moral and scientific clichés of the newspaper or the complications of *Huppim and Muppim and Ard,* if only they would give us instruction in the history and philosophy of our religion, in the technique of our art—religious art, the art of our intercourse with

[134]

the unseen—then there is a chance that we should pass from these vain struggles in the sand to the peace and opportunity of the house built upon the rock.

In conclusion, let them give us more of God. Let us hear less of "values" and more of Him without Whom all values are bankrupt and worthless. It is possible in these days of Christian civilization to live a moral life without Christ, but we ought to be too proud to draw thus upon the bank of the Saints. Christianity still requires a man to sell all that he hath—all his safe inheritance of good conduct, good nature, and good form—and enter naked on the personal and penniless adventure of the love of God.

THE IMPORTANCE OF STYLE

by Dr. Henry Seidel Canby

The Importance of Style

By Dr. Henry Seidel Canby

THE English Bible is dying. I do not mean its theology nor its historical or spiritual content. I do not refer to the controversies between Fundamentalists and Rationalists, nor to the interpretation as poetry and legend of what once was regarded as literal fact. Where the Bible is historical at all there is probably more evidence as to its historicity available than ever before. I do not assert that its moral values have declined, although they have certainly been transvalued, nor that as great literature it is one whit less than our ancestors (when they dared to think of it as literature at all) believed it.

But all qualifications aside, the English Bible, and specifically the King James version, is losing, or has already lost, a power over the imagination almost unexampled in history. It was couched in a prose so rich with the genius of a great language, and so invariably read with reverence, love, or fear, that there is perhaps no equivalent instance of the style as well as the substance of a single book influencing and sometimes dominating the mold of thought and form of expression of a whole people.

The Bible, for English speakers from the seventeenth century on, was the Word. When they read "The Word was made flesh, and dwelt among us," they thought, or should have thought, of Christ as the Divine Intelligence and Mediator between God and man. But it was the English phrase, not the Greek meaning, which prevailed. The Logos, for English readers, was neither reason nor the Divine expression as such, but the Word of a sacred Book, authoritative, irrefutable, magic. And it was a great Word. The most sophisticated megalopolitan cannot read Isaiah today, or Paul, without yielding to the spell. There has been equal eloquence in other tongues, but no such prevailing eloquence. Not all the obscurities, the contradictions, and the absurdities in the Bible can detract from its great power in this respect. Enter to scoff and you remain to be stirred and exalted.

My argument is simple and must be simply stated. Whatever the spiritual and theological strength of the English Bible, its influence was due in no slight measure to the power of English eloquence, to style in the truest sense of the word. Whatever else it may have been, it was a great Book, a strong Word, an inescapable pressure of great statement, vital, simple, beautiful, upon ordinary man. If he did not read Homer, Vergil, Dante, Shakespeare, Milton, Addison, Wordsworth, Keats, Emerson, Whitman, he had this. And if the subject-matter of the Bible had been the Hindu Gospel or Greek mythology or Buddhism or the philosophy of Confucius, and if the English style had possessed like qualities of excellence, the influence for which I am arguing would still have been immense.

There is an interesting parallel in Fitzgerald's "Rubáiyát" of Omar Khayyám, a poem more Fitzgerald's than Omar's, yet expressing a philosophy sharply different from the ordinary currents of English thinking, and nevertheless couched in such vital English as to become the most widely quoted poetry of the latter nineteenth century.

It is as the Word, in the sense which English readers understood, that the English Bible is dying. It is through this Word, whether spoken or written, that we got our strongest moral and spiritual stimulus. The power of a phrase may, and often does, exceed the power of an idea, because the phrase may carry with it a train of emotional suggestion and a stir to reminiscence that moves the whole being:

I am the resurrection, and the life: he that believeth in me, though he were dead, yet shall he live: and whosoever liveth and believeth in me, shall never die.

Out of the deep have I called unto thee, O Lord: Lord, hear my voice. O let thine ears consider well: the voice of my complaint. If thou, Lord, wilt be extreme to mark what is done amiss: O Lord, who may abide it.

And in the Biblical tradition:

Almighty God, who hast given us grace at this time with one accord to make our common supplications unto thee, and dost promise that when two or three are gathered together in thy Name thou wilt grant their requests; Fulfil now, O Lord, the desires and petitions of thy servants, as may be most expedient for them; granting us in this world knowledge of thy truth, and in the world to come life everlasting.

From the Word in this sense our religious life has been quickened and the mind exalted. Not the literal meaning, but the rich suggestiveness of the phrase has been a saving help in time of trouble or the cause of new realization or resolve. The letter killeth, but the spirit giveth life, can be very fairly paraphrased into a literary statement of the power of the Word.

At the moment when words have been given wings to speak round the world, when the radio has increased the stature (but unfortunately not the mind) of the orator by a cubit, so that where he spoke to a thousand, now a million hear him; when the press and its reduplications pour words in a torrent over every mind, the Word, as our ancestors knew it, has lost its power, speaks no more with final authority even to the most devout, and as a factor in spiritual and æsthetic education has become quaint and reminiscent rather than vital and awesome. Whatever statistics may show as to the sales and distribution of the English Bible, it is not read as it once was. Our daily conversation, our writing, and our speaking prove this too readily. Ye shall know them by their fruits applies to books as well as to men. Even Fundamentalists are modern (shall we say, most modern) in their colloquial spoken style, and if the Bible is read weekly in churches, it is clear that neither preacher nor congregation listen as they once listened to the Word.

I belong, myself, to that Quakerish school that never made a fetish of the Bible, and should be particularly disinclined to argue for a return to the general, indiscriminate, daily reading of the Bible which once was common. Not even the seventeenth century could turn all the Bible into impressive prose. Revelation is tedious and hysterical when it is not magnificent. Old Testament ethics are frequently shocking, and the English of certain speeches of Jehovah and Jeremiah is much more admirable than their content or the character of the speakers.

Nor do I hold with the worthy teachers who would have us adopt the English Bible as a model for current English. That is, to speak brusquely, nonsense. The Biblical style is eloquent and almost unequaled in emotional expressiveness. But it is entirely inadequate for exact statement or lucid analysis, as indeed was all English prose before the eighteenth century. The revision of revised versions has made its obscurer passages clearer only by a descent into flat modernism which sacrifices rhythm and emotion to the meaning of the original. This great style rises to its height, as all agree, in the Old Testament, where it is precisely least adapted to the

[144]

needs of a scientific age, to any age, indeed, not content to express itself by poetical indirection.

The rules of logical English composition are nearly all broken in the Bible. Unity is by no means constant, coherence is casual, only emphasis is invariably maintained. To urge a youth entering any department of modern life to form his style upon the Bible is as foolish as to advise tilting, camelriding, and the study of medicinal herbs as a preparation for engineering or the law. The English style of the Bible is more remote from the practical necessities of modern prose than Pindar from the exposition of Aristotle. It is a magnificent prose, but absolutely unadapted to the expression of nine-tenths of what we as journalists, scientists, novelists, legalists, scholars, and even ministers must necessarily express.

It is as a stimulant, a corrective, and a source, that the Biblical style has been so valuable. Lincoln did not learn to write from the Bible. He learned to write from Blackstone and the historians and the essayists. His Gettysburg speech is not Biblical in its style, but eighteenth century at the earliest. It was from the Bible that he learned pitch, and exaltation, and the power of the word. It was his reading and hearing of the Bible that gave him simplicity and force in his diction. Order, clarity, logic, accuracy—these indispensables of style in a modern civilization—he got elsewhere.

Thus it is not to be deplored that editorial writers in the London or the New York *Times* do not use the style of Jeremiah. If they did, we would not read them; indeed, we know too well, from a familiar kind of sermon, the unfortunate results of talking seventeenth century when you have a twentieth (or late nineteenth!) century brain. Yet it is to be regretted that we do not have what Lincoln had, nor are ever likely to possess it in the same measure from the same source. For the attitude of awed reverence for the Bible is gone, and what is more important, the wide and continual and often exclusive reading of the Bible is gone. The Word will always have power, but the power of a classic not a Scripture. It will never again lift with little effort the style of plain men like John Bunyan or George Fox, because it is no longer in the active consciousness of plain men that read and listen. Norman French, with a great literature behind it, died out in England because the speakers could not count on an understanding. The parallel is inexact because there are elements of permanence in the English Bible and factors of resemblance in modern English not present in the analogue, but the comparison points my meaning. The Bible and Biblical English will stay, will enrich our style, will stir our emotions (is it conceivable that the story of Absalom will ever lose its poignancy?), but the Word as an influence of privileged might and universal acceptance is dying. It may put on the immortality of literature, but its moral dominance is gone.

I come—to quote from that other great reservoir of English style—to bury Cæsar, not to praise him. My preaching is concerned not so much with holding fast to our inheritance in the English Bible, as with inevitable losses that already may be estimated and are likely to increase. For with the decline of the majestic influence of Jacobean prose a whole department of style seems to be lost to us, and to regard the loss as merely literary is to take a most superficial view.

It may be said that the current age is scientific, utilitarian, practical, and therefore needs only the plain and flexible, simple and accurate prose which it is getting in characteristic specimens from our best writers. But this generalization is not true, and if it were, no one could rest content with what it implies.

We are scientific, utilitarian, practical, and we do need and have got in our modern English an instrument almost as accurate and flexible as French prose, and probably more expressive. To write now like Ruskin or Carlyle or Dr. Johnson or Robert Burton or the makers of the English Bible is a sign of weakness, not strength, and (whatever teachers of English and Tory critics may say) that kind of writing for us is nothing, gets nowhere, and indicates more surely than anything else a spiritual and æsthetic plagiarism. It is well known among teachers of English that one of the surest symptoms of the intellectual parasitism of a second-rate mind is an essay written in the style of Charles Lamb.

But not all of us, and no one of us, is all scientific, utilitarian, practical. These are merely the contours which are turned for touch and shaping to this age in which we live. The waters still run deep even though the angel of the Old Testament seldom troubles them. A craving for beauty, a sense of awe, a moral urge, the love of an ideal, the need of worship, the belief in spiritual values, are of course as existent in a machine age as in any other. They have not pressed for expression because other needs in this economic century have been more urgent, and still more perhaps because the expressiveness of our fathers has until recently been sufficient for traits temporarily recessive. But they must find expression somehow, and may need a new expressiveness at any moment more urgently than do the measurements of science. Science, indeed, having come close to metaphysics, needs a new diction now. The physicist falls from very helplessness into the language of the Bible in the attempt to intimate (for he cannot express) his new sense of the non-existence of mere things.

It seems that we need a new Bible—new Jobs, new Pauls, new Isaiahs, but not in their similitudes nor with their voices. I do not refer to a new theology, although that is inevitable, nor to new spiritual and ethical conceptions, although they too are inevitable in so far as anything spiritual and ethical can be new. I mean a new responsibility for the Word as eloquence—as the "speaking out" of the depths of man. This means in plain English a new expressiveness for what is not practical, utilitarian, scientific, and sophisticated.

The King James version was a new medium for expression. I am naturally aware that it was a translation, and also of its partial dependence on earlier versions as far back as Wycliffe. Nevertheless, it stands of itself; it dates as of seventeenth-century Protestant England where the leadership of the New World was being forged. The interpenetration of its language through all serious English literature of the next centuries is proof of what was accomplished. A new eloquence for spiritual and ethical concepts was given to the race. The subject-matter was not English, although it deeply concerned the England of the day, but the style was native.

It may be done again, though not in the same way. It may be done, not for an ancient Scripture, but for some new subject of quest and craving. It must be done. We must translate deep spiritual emotion and strong, ethical desires into our vernacular, but first from the vernacular we must make or remake a style.

The psychological effect of reading, as reading goes today, is difficult to estimate, but must be extraordinary. The book, as Spengler says with his customary dogmatism, but at least an aspect of truth, is disappearing. For the masses, who no longer are illiterate, this is the age of reading—of newspaper and magazine reading—and of hearing the same kind of journalism over the radio. Millions of words, flat and soggy most of them, fall like an endless snow upon civilized man. He is drifted in with them, buried; wherever he goes he wades through printed or spoken words. His business is by words said or words read, and in his leisure he opens his mind to them. At the least estimate a city dweller reads or hears fifty thousand words a day.

This circumstance is so new that we can only guess at an outcome. That our thoughts are increasingly formulated in words—words drifted into the mind—is probable. That we use words more and get less from them seems certain. The commonplaceness of everyday living in modern comfort is in part a mental reaction to the flatness of the words in which we have our being. Tabloid readers will eventually talk and think in tabloid—a soggy sensationalism. The mind overfed on the style so bleached of color and strained of disturbing complexities which is the ideal of good journalism and reaches its perfection of nullity in the English of radio broadcasting, will have no other medium in which to express itself. And the modern prose of literary masters which I, for one, admire, a prose that is adroit, accurate, subtle, scientific in the best sense, is still inadequate for purposes that must even in a prosaic age be importunate. It would be impossible to translate into its skillful common sense the religious emotions of Job:

Who is this that darkeneth counsel by words without knowledge? Gird up now thy loins like a man; for I will demand of thee, and answer thou me. Where wast thou when I laid the foundations of the earth? declare, if thou hast understanding. Who hath laid the measures thereof, if thou knowest? Or who hath stretched the line upon it? Whereupon are the foundations thereof fastened? or who laid the cornerstone thereof; when the morning stars sang together, and all the sons of God shouted for joy? Or who shut up the sea with doors, when it brake forth as if it had issued out of the womb? When I made the cloud the garment thereof, and thick darkness a swaddlingband for it, and brake up for it my decreed place, and set bars and doors, and said, Hitherto shalt thou come, but no further: and here shall thy proud waves be stayed? . . . Have the gates of death been opened unto thee? or hast thou seen the doors of the shadow of death? . . . Canst thou bind the sweet influences of Pleiades, or loose the bands of Orion? Canst thou bring forth Mazzaroth in his season? or canst thou guide Arcturus with his sons? Knowest thou the ordinances of heaven? Canst thou set the dominion thereof in the earth? . . . Gird up thy loins now like a man: I will demand of thee, and declare thou unto me.

And who dares to say that our inability to find equivalent organ tones of English is because we have no religious emotion, no spiritual insight, no quests and no cravings as urgent, if less naïve, than Job's to express!

Modern English is lacking in eloquence, in its root sense of speaking out and its acquired meaning of speaking out from the heart. We need a new "grand style," and it is not a sufficient answer to say that first we must acquire grandeur. For grandeur is a constant, relative only in its degree and its manifestations, and in literature truly limited by the ability of an age to express its inner self. In this country we were well on the way to attain a prose style with scope and lift, in the creative period of the American imagination which ended with the Civil War. Emerson and Thoreau were both eloquent, and Thoreau, at least, wrote with a mind as modern as our own. There has been little real eloquence in American prose since because there has been little felt need. And should a prophet arrive, or, if that is too archaic a term, a great teacher, philosopher, preacher, or writer of Pascal's caliber or Milton's,

[153]

where is his medium? Can he forge it overnight? It was a group of quite undistinguished men, as literature goes, who made the English Bible. But they had a great prose ready at hand.

It is hard to write of a Great Need without falling into the bombast or abstraction of those who speak of Long Felt Wants and Next Steps and Urgent Duties. This sermon on style raises, of course, more questions than it answers, and indeed that is my purpose. It implies, for example, that literature with a purpose deserves a great style, and this is an idea very distasteful to modern critics who like to see the cool detachment of science extended to art. Description, measurement, analysis, have been at the heart of twentieth-century literature. Writers who attempted other modes have been called propagandists, sentimentalists, or accused (often rightly) of stale romantic symbolism.

And yet, though ethics has been run out of poetry and fiction clipped of its morals, the didactic has merely changed its costume for a business suit and sneaked back by the stage door in Shaw's plays or entered as a hard-boiled journalist in H. G. Wells's novels.

The difference between H. G. Wells and the Bible

can be measured in style. Both preach morality, and while I am not comparing subject-matters, I am willing to grant to Wells a rather exalted morality. But Wells has no eloquence and needs none for his appeals to common sense.

There is, indeed, always a moral, and a religious literature, too, being written, even in the most immoral societies. But if we insist upon it being unliterary, not eloquent, deny it beauty and the attributes of art, turn it over to the journalists and the satirists and the professional propagandists, we get the kind of style and the kind of literature for which we ask. Even then, a Hardy will take a scientific age on its own terms and make great poetry of its doubts.

But it is not enough to say that we get the style we deserve. I readily grant that a commonplace people, let us say the Dutch of the eighteenth century, are not going to produce masterpieces of literary art. But where are the critics wise enough to estimate the essential greatness or littleness of their own times! It is argued that this is the great and virile age of America. It is argued that we are in the very decadence of true Americanism. Let them argue. All that can safely be said until time has finished with us, is that our literature is more or less expressive of what we are. The Elizabethan literature, it is now clear, was immensely expressive; the writing of the mauve decade of the recent 'nineties, when the astonishing twentieth century was in full preparation, was certainly not very expressive, or fully expressive only of imperialism, a fine-drawn febrile æsthetics, and a vague romantic sentimentalism destined to blow away like mist banks within a decade.

Our styles—the adroit sophisticated style of the subtler British novelists and poets, the plain man-to-man style of Wells and Sinclair Lewis, the colorless, but readable and fluent style of American journalism, smart, humorous, and often wise in the columnists, informative, unemotional, but pointed and close to human needs in the *Saturday Evening Post* or the *New York Times,* the familiar, colloquial style of realistic poetry and modern biographical writing—these styles are all expressive and some of them excellent instruments. No one wants sex novels written in the prose of the Song of Solomon or articles on the plan of II Corinthians. Journalists and novelists alike have done well by the English language. They can say what they want and say it as well as it has ever been said. But who shall assert that there are no profounder emotions, neither descriptive nor analytic, demanding a different and nobler style in prose and poetry than any of these? And if they exist, by what tongue shall they speak?

My somewhat ideal thesis, therefore, is that we must recapture the Word, with all the content I have tried to give to that term. We are in real danger of losing, in an age of flat prose, an essential and invaluable capacity of the language, fully realized once in the English Bible, but realizable again—the capacity to express by tone and overtone, by rhythm, and by beauty and force of vocabulary, the religious, the spiritual, the ethical cravings of man who would still be obsessed by them if he were proved—as now seems most unlikely—to be only a biological machine.

And the Word, while secondary if you will, and an instrument only, is indispensable for turning ideas and emotions into communicable force. If, as the eighteenth century naïvely believed, we could find all that we need to say in the classics, if we could rest finally content with the eloquence of Job! But their words are already dim for a generation that does not feel their authority or receive their connotations; and such styles cannot voice the strange vicissitudes of an age that knows the mysteries of the prophets are the commonplaces of science, and yet must face new mysteries more perplexing and less absolute.

Who will give us a new Bible in English? For to one sensitive to the power of language, and aware of the difference between words and the Word, the priests of the twentieth century babble in a jargon that has lost its vitality, and the prophets are tongue-tied with a language that can say everything but what they most deeply feel and mean. They have the tongues of men, but not angels; not even sounding brass and tinkling cymbals, but only a language of the machine that can go swiftly to the right and to the left, but never up.

BEHIND THE VEIL OF DEATH

by Sir A. Conan Doyle

Behind the Veil of Death

By Sir A. Conan Doyle

IF I had just one chance to preach I believe that
I could best show my appreciation of the opportunity by giving forth that which I believe to be
true, and which I am assured represents the religious knowledge of the future, even if for the
moment it should be unpopular or misunderstood.
Religion cannot always stand still, or be referred
eternally to documents thousands of years old, many
of which are far below our modern standards of
intelligence and morality. God still yearns over the
world which He has created, and He still from time
to time, as it is ready to receive it, transmits to it
by this or that chosen and inspired messenger fresh
knowledge by which man may know something of
his destiny. I believe that within the last eighty
years a flood of such knowledge has been conveyed
to us, and that we have been extraordinarily blind
as to its validity and its overwhelming importance.

So convinced am I of the vital nature of this psychic knowledge, that I have been gradually forced to the conclusion that it is the most important event which has occurred in the world since that raising of ethical standards which we associate with the revered name of Jesus of Nazareth, and that on the plane of religious knowledge, as apart from ethics, it is actually the most important even of any.

For consider what it means if it be true. We claim that we can break through the barrier of death, that those who have lived in this world have not changed either their forms or their characters, but only their vibrations, so that instead of manifesting through the flesh body, which is a low and slow vibration, they live now in an etheric body which is on a high and fast vibration, and therefore invisible to our ordinary mortal eyes, exactly as many things in our daily life fail to impress our senses because they are on too fast a vibration. Colors beyond the spectrum and notes above our compass are examples of what I mean. These etheric bodies do not, as we learn, live in a vacuum or in any indefinite state, but they pass from this earth into a more complex, but as a rule a far higher, society, in which they have definite duties and congenial work in which

[162]

they have every chance of developing to the full their own natural powers, as well as of enjoying those things which give them natural pleasure. We learn also that the bond of sympathy and affection is the one permanent thing which regulates the re-uniting or the sundering of those who have been in contact with each other down here, and that happy reassembled households are usual there, with all elements of discord removed.

If this were all that we brought to mankind, what a gigantic step forward—what an enormous advance of knowledge would it represent! It is the unknown nature of death and its severance of all our ties which cast a shadow upon our lives. But if we know that all is natural, that there is nothing to fear, and that our love ties are not broken, then what a load is lifted! It is strange indeed to think that this inestimable gift which we bring has been so misrepresented by our enemies, that one would really imagine that it was something blasphemous or obscene which we were forcing upon the human race. The responsibility of the churches in this matter is enormous, and it is not too much to say that the apathy and ignorance concerning this spiritual knowledge which is shown among many of the

[163]

leaders of religion is as discreditable as it is hard
to understand. Surely they, of all men, should be
the first to meet us, since we bring them actual proofs
of personal survival, and of so much else which they
have themselves affirmed. For centuries they have
been worsted in their fight with the skeptics who
very reasonably demand proofs instead of tests. We
at last bring them those proofs, so that they can
meet the scientist upon his own ground, but instead
of recognition or gratitude, nothing but the coldest
of receptions has been accorded us. This is not bad
for us, since we stand upon our own feet, but it is
fatal for the churches which turn away from that
spiritual help and inspiration which God's new revelation brings with it.

Where does that spiritual help come in? It comes
in from the fact that we can use our new powers
not only to get into touch with our own loved ones,
who may perhaps be on no higher a level of character and knowledge than we are ourselves, but also,
when we are worthy, we get clear messages from
those who are in a far more spiritual condition than
ourselves and are indeed what, under the old dis-
pensation, would be called high angels. From these
direct communications a flood of spiritual knowl-

edge has come into the world, all of it, as it seems to us, of a beautiful and rational nature. We do not accept such statements blindly. We are not fanatics or visionaries. We weigh the messages with our own God-given reason, and we admit the fact that the medium through whom the message passes may well color it with his own personality and beliefs. But none the less, making every allowance for this, the messages are so consistent and on so high a level that they have, as it seems to us, as good a claim to be a divine inspiration as anything which has ever reached the world in the past.

We have many reasons for thinking that this flood of information is truly supernormal. The first is that it has been accompanied by a vast body of signs which have been clearly supernormal. Much of this evidence has been physical, consisting of those phenomena which have been tested and confirmed by tens of thousands of hard-headed observers, including many notable men of science. Let him who denies this statement read the evidence carefully before he dares to repeat the denial. Much of the evidence, too, comes from mental phenomena, independent of the darkness of the séance room, when great numbers of credible witnesses attest that they have come

[165]

in contact with intelligences which have been able to give them complete tests that they are indeed the souls of those whom they had known and who have left this sphere. This enormous volume of evidence, which is recorded in hundreds of books, cannot be pooh-poohed or waved aside. It is there, and it is a portentous fact, which agrees closely with what we learn of the signs of the spirit as recorded of old.

This is one reason for regarding our philosophy as supernatural. The second is that the explanation of the true scheme of the universe has come from a vast number of independent sources, many of which could by no means have been influenced by the others, and that, with some small exceptions, there is a truly remarkable agreement running through them. These messages have come from children, from uneducated people, from all sorts of sources, including, in one case for which I can answer, a confirmed skeptic who was made an involuntary instrument for writing down the truth. If three or four witnesses who agree can gain the verdict of an earthly court, then why should these thousands who have recorded the same story not gain credence in the court of the world? This is so obvious that it is only apathy and ignorance of the facts which prevent its acceptance.

But the final argument for the truth of our new revelation is that it is the most natural, reasonable, and comforting interpretation of the facts of human life and destiny which has ever been put forward. It is huge, sweeping, all-explaining, reaching out to all our difficulties, and giving adequate answers.

Whence, then, did it come? Is it to be imagined that the little group of uneducated people who received the first inspirations were themselves the inventors of this great sweeping explanation of the universe? Is it to be thought that a man like Jackson Davis, who was perhaps the recipient of as much of the new knowledge as anyone, was the inventor of this knowledge, he being a man who was entirely illiterate at the time? Such ideas are absurd. If the philosophy did not come from external supernatural prompting, then whence did it come?

There are, then, three tests. The first is the signs which have been given to us. The second is the uniformity and consistency of the messages. The third is the reasonable nature of the whole philosophy, which it is above human wit to invent and which does not correspond with any other philosophy which preceded it. I hold that these three considerations are overwhelming ones, and that we have no excuse at all if we fail to take the matter seriously.

Now let us look a little more carefully at what it is that we have gained. I have already alluded to the fact that our natural fear of death is removed. We learn from those who have been down the path before us, that though the illness which leads to death may be a severe trial, death itself is a sweet and pleasant languor, akin to that of the tired body dropping to sleep, and that it is made the easier in that the etheric eyes become clearer, while the bodily ones fade, and that we are aware of the smiling faces, and of the outstretched hands of those whom we would most love to see again. We are assured of this by many who have passed, and we have the clear corroboration of many death-bed phenomena. A few of these, a very few, have been clearly recorded in that valuable little book *Death-Bed Visions* by the late Sir William Barrett, a man whose keen and skeptical scientific intelligence was quite convinced by the facts laid before him.

But here for a moment we must distinguish. Who are these kindly souls who meet the quivering spirit at the moment when it most needs help and guidance? All agree that they are those who love us. But if we have not won love, how can they be there? Who is there to meet the cruel man, the selfish man, the man who has lived for himself alone? There are no parasites or sycophants over there. Wealth and temporal power are gone. As a famous spirit said bitterly to me once, "We do not carry our check-books over. We have been so busy over the things which do not matter that we have neglected the things that do matter!" For such people it is a bleak and lonely moment, for they have begun to reap the harvest which they have sown. I will revert presently to what we know of the sad fate of such undeveloped souls, who are not the lowly of earth, but very often those of the greatest wealth and of the highest intelligence, who have not used that wealth and intelligence for God's purposes, or have perhaps allowed their brains to grow at the expense of their hearts. I will for the moment follow the fortunes of what I may call the average kindly man or woman, when released into their etheric life.

We are told that things follow each other in a very natural sequence. For a short period he is congratulated and reassured by the friends around him,

[169]

and it is during that short time that his thoughts flash back often to those that he has left, and that he can, as so often happens, make some sort of telepathic impression upon their minds. These visions at the time, or just after death, make quite a literature of their own, so that to that extent we corroborate from this side what they tell us from their own experience. Then for a time there is rest.

This rest would appear to be of a longer or shorter duration according to the need of the individual. When it is over he finds the same kind guardians by his side who will introduce him to the glories and the duties of the new world which await him.

I have already spoken of the natural and, if I may use the word, homely nature of this new life. To us the spirit body and its surroundings may appear to be vaporous, unsubstantial things. But that is a misconception. If people who lived in a world of lead looked upon our world it would seem to be light and vaporous. It all depends upon the comparison between the body and its surroundings. If these are all to scale, then the spirit body finds the world around it just as real and solid as we do ours. When this is realized, all our difficulties about the shadowy ghost disappear. You get a false standard

[170]

if you compare the things of one sphere with those of another. You must judge their condition by their own environment.

We have now got to the stage where the freed spirit goes forth into his new life. It is inconceivably beautiful in externals and the soul is happy with such a deep satisfying happiness as this world cannot give. He is with those he loves and all jarring elements have been removed. His home has been prepared for him by the loving hands of those who preceded him. It is just as he would like it to be. His own tastes have in all matters been consulted. He finds flowers and gardens, woods and streams, all illuminated by a golden radiance. Soon he is offered a choice of duties so that he may use his natural powers in the best way. Where he has several powers his vocation may be as hard to find as it often is here. Thus Lester Coltman in his posthumous description of the life beyond had to choose between music and science, eventually choosing science as his study and music as his recreation. There, as here, facilities are provided for the work in hand, libraries for the scholar, laboratories for the man of science, temples, lecture rooms, centers for dramatic, artistic, and musical education. All these matters are pushed, they declare, far farther than with us—indeed, our own developments are merely reflections from above.

For the children we read of delightful playing fields, simple, innocent pleasures, education under the most charming conditions. A mother will mourn the physical absence of her dead child, but when she knows what we can tell her the tears will be dried and the heart uplifted as she realizes all that the child has gained and all that it has been spared.

The religious sense is awakened and stimulated by the glories which surround the new-born soul. His love and adoration increase when it is understood how infinitely kind the Creator has been, and when the riddle of Life's apparent injustices and cruelties has been partially solved. And yet it is not a life of monotonous devotion. There, as here, they should have God in their hearts, but life itself is a round of domestic peace and useful congenial labor.

Such is the picture of the other life which we have received from the other side—in its most favorable aspect. Is there anything unnatural in it? Is it, on the face of it, improbable? All evolution is gradual and we can well understand that the soul

[172]

cannot at once be altered by its disengagement from the body. It carries with it the same tastes and aspirations, and it is reasonable, therefore, to suppose that the means of gratifying them is there. Is the artist to be cut off from his art, or the musician from his music, or the literary man from his expression when in each case it is the man's very self, and if you took it away he would indeed be another individual? Such a supposition revolts our reason. But if all these arts are practiced, then an audience is also predicated, and thus one gets a glimpse of the reality of that happy community.

Do not suppose that this semi-material heaven is a final one. Nothing is final. We grow and grow through the ages. But at least it is the next step, and it is so happy a step that we may well be satisfied, even if other glories await us beyond. It is the compensation for the troubles of life; it is the rest house after the journey; it is the fulfillment of God's promises and the justification of all his dealings with the human race.

So much for the fate of the deserving people who are really the vast majority of the human race. All this talk of our being naturally wicked, and always plunged in sin, is perfect nonsense. When one has

[173]

subtracted all the sin which is due to circumstances, to environment, to heredity, the balance is not so very serious. The human race has been far too modest about its own achievement. Most people make a brave, good fight amid all the disabilities which have to be faced, and instead of punishment they deserve what they get, and that is reward and compensation.

But we cannot deny the existence of evil—of real evil which is within our own control. There is selfishness, that is the root of nearly all flaws of character. There is cruelty, and nothing brings such retribution as that. Physical cruelty may be rare, but mental cruelty—the cruelty of the bitter speech, of the ill-natured gossip, is very common. That brings its own punishment. Then there is bigotry, which is really a form of cruelty, since it is confining God's mercy to a chosen few. And there is pride, which again rises from selfishness. Surely a conceited person standing under the arch of the Milky Way is the most absurd object in nature. Then beyond all this there is the brutish mind, the mind which has no spirituality in it, the mind which has been entirely engrossed in the things of this world, successful perhaps in worldly success, but paying the price that it is sunk in the mud of the world until it cannot disengage itself. There are the various types which suffer in the beyond.

We must make a distinction as to the form of suffering. There is the person who is tied to earth by his earthly interests. He is like an airplane which is too heavy to rise into the air. It lingers upon or near the surface of that world toward which its mind is turned. These are the earthbound spirits, an enormous assembly, millions and millions of them, a few here and there so near to matter that they actually impinge upon our material senses and are seen by us as phantoms. The miser is held by his gold, the man of intellect by his study, the monk by his cell, the criminal by his crime, the merchant by his ledger. All whose thoughts have been utterly engrossed by the world are to be found there, many of them unable to realize that they are dead. At our rescue circles they ridicule the idea that they are dead. For centuries they may remain as in some vague nightmare. Then at last realization comes and that is the beginning of regeneration. Those who have read the posthumous writings of Oscar Wilde and of Jack London will realize the position and emotions of the spirit who is conscious that he is earthbound.

Then apart from the earthbound, the existence of whom is testified to by the experience and traditions of all ages and nations, we have those who have passed on into true spirit life, but who are conscious of their own shortcomings upon earth. How low some of these may fall and how acute their punishment may be is a matter upon which we are not clearly informed. There is reason to think that there is a lowest stratum of evil beings whose fate is not far different from that of the hell of the Scriptures, save, indeed, that there is always at long last the hope of amelioration of soul and therefore of condition. Above there are other strata of whose fate we know more. These are heavy-hearted at the thought of their own failure, and their condition seems to correspond with their mental and spiritual state, so that they are for the time in dim and cloudy places where dreary surroundings match the dreary thoughts within. There they must linger until sooner or later their own conscience or some ministering angel comes to give them that upward help which is the beginning of their regeneration. It would seem to be a sad state while it lasts, but only by sorrow and pain do chastening and amendment come, as we may see so often in our ordinary human life. How intolerable often is the human being who has known no sorrow! Only by it does he learn sympathy and understanding.

So much we are told of the next stage of existence. Again I would ask, is it in any way incredible or unreasonable? Is it not more reasonable, for example, than that one should lie inert for countless ages until some judgment should come? Is it not also more reasonable than the idea of a heaven of adoration, for which we are by no means fitted, or of an endless hell, which, as it did not amend the soul, could only serve the purpose of divine revenge? And yet these are the schemes of after-life existence which so many generations have found themselves able to accept. The present philosophy, too, is not drawn from witnesses long dead or from chronicles which can never be retranslated without copious errors being discovered, and never examined without fresh forgeries and interpolations being suspected, but they are messages direct to ourselves, of a far higher morality than that of these ancient tribes, and fortified by preternatural signs which show their other-world origin. These high teachings profess to come

[177]

from lofty spirits who have gained wisdom in the beyond. Their beauty and dignity bear out the claim. If it be said that such messages cannot be proved to be from such a source, one can only reply that at least the proof is as clear, or even clearer, than it has ever been in the past history of the world.

How does such teaching react upon Christianity? It does not in any way touch upon the ethics of Christ. I have, if I may for a moment be personal, had more beautiful messages about the teaching and personality of Christ from my own guide Pheneas than I have ever had or heard of from any other source. But there is nothing narrow in such messages. There is nothing which makes the monstrous claim that God supports one clique of mankind against another. Always the teaching is that belief and faith are small matters beside character and behavior, that it is these latter which determine the place of the soul in the beyond. Every faith, Christian or non-Christian, has its saints and its sinners, and if a man be kindly and gentle there is no fear for him in the beyond whether he is or is not the member of any recognized Church on earth.

Those well-meaning folk in the Christian churches who shrink away from this new knowledge because it *is* new, must remember that there is outside their churches a vast assembly of men in every country, often as earnest as themselves, who have been so abashed by the degenerate religion which they see around them that they have lost all belief either in a God or in the survival after death. It is to these people that spiritualism has often come as a light in the darkness. They have longed for some firm spot of ground in the quagmire of the faiths, where every creed has its own interpretations, and they have found that firm spot—the only one which my foot has ever found—in the philosophy of Spiritualism, which may start in a lowly atmosphere of puerile phenomena but leads upward step by step in an unbroken line of experience and reason until it reaches an elevation too rarefied for the human mind. Even this life extends from the hooligan to the saint, and can we wonder that the next presents similar extremes all within the same system of thought?

I have finished. One cannot in a single short discourse do more than sketch the outlines. Reading and experience must supply the details. But I would end as I began in emphasizing the extraordinary overmastering importance of the matter. Three great things have happened in the history of the human race, things so permanent that the mere rise and fall of empires is as nothing in comparison. The first is the idea of a single God in the universe. The second is the idea of the unselfish code of morals which may be found in many places but which we mainly associate with Jesus of Nazareth—a code which distinguishes man from beast. The third is the breaking of the veil which separates our sphere of life from the next one. It is at this last tremendous revelation that we now assist. Blessed is he who is privileged to forward the manifest work of God. Take heed, take heed, how you resist Him.

THE THREE VOICES OF NATURE
by Prof. J. Arthur Thomson, LL.D.

The Three Voices of Nature

By Prof. J. Arthur Thomson, LL.D.

"And a great and strong wind rent
the mountains, and brake in pieces the
rocks before the Lord; but the Lord
was not in the wind: and after the
wind an earthquake; but the Lord was
not in the earthquake: and after the
earthquake a fire; but the Lord was
not in the fire: and after the fire a still
small voice" (or a sound of gentle
stillness).

—I. KINGS, XIX:11-12.

THERE is nothing very fanciful in speaking of nature's voices. For even those among us who refuse
to admit that Nature has a divine purpose, or that
this includes being an encouragement and a warning to man, will admit that we may learn something
from Nature. Even those who refuse to be other
than "strictly scientific"—an unnecessarily self-
denying ordinance—must admit that Nature is an

[183]

experimental station on a grand scale, where living creatures are experimented with, and there must be something here for our instruction. Organic evolution is a long-drawn-out drama, continued for hundreds of millions of years, and we must be dull indeed if we can find no lessons to be learned from the age-long advances and retrogressions, extinctions and efflorescences. In the first instance we mean by "voices" that the evolving system of Nature has hints which man can use to his advantage.

The idea of voices of Nature to be listened to becomes less cold and distant when we bear in mind that man, according to science, is the outcome of long-continued natural processes of varying and entailing, sifting and singling. Willy-nilly he is Nature's child. He must be very deaf if he thinks his *alma mater* dumb. Furthermore, since man began to become man, he has been trafficking with Nature, sometimes yielding to her stern pressure, sometimes rebelling vigorously, following one trend of evolution and then another, now imitating and again reversing Nature's ways. When we recognize not only man's place in Nature, but his commerce with Nature for good and ill for many thousands of years, we cannot but discern some way posts and danger sig-

[184]

nals. Man transcends Nature, but he has much to learn from her ways.

The atmosphere changes when we find, necessarily outside of science, some good reasons for begging the greatest of all questions, and postulate religiously a divine significance in Nature, whose mundane crown man is. For if Nature is Nature for a purpose, and if the fulfillment of part of that purpose is man, then it is no longer fanciful to think of Nature as a revelation, seeking to make itself heard, if haply man will hearken. Thus *vox naturae* may become *vox Dei.*

Since man has a threefold relation to Nature—practical, emotional, and intellectual—we have spoken of the *three* voices; but there might be five, or seven, or even nine. We mean strong impulses that come to man because of the cords that bind him to Nature—the system of things and beings of which he forms a part and from which he has emerged. We mean the wordless voices referred to in the XIXth Psalm: "The heavens declare the glory of God and the firmament showeth His handiwork." Day unto day is welling forth speech, and night unto night is breathing out knowledge; there is indeed no speech, and there are no words; their voice has no audible sound; yet it resonates over all the earth. It seems to us that the three great voices of Nature are—Endeavor, Enjoy, Inquire.

When the Hebrew prophet listened to the voices of Nature, the first he heard was the *wind*—a symbol of the appeal to the practical side of man. What it says is Endeavor. For it is the wind that tells the sailor when to furl and unfurl his sails, that tells the husbandman when to gather in his harvest lest it be scattered, that tells the builder to lay his foundations well so that the house may stand four-square to the storms. In some ways this is Nature's loudest voice—for it is the voice of the struggle for existence. For millions of years there has been stern sifting for health, for vigor, for efficiency, for masterfulness. Of course there are evasions such as parasitism, which Nature may be said to tolerate, though usually marking with dishonor-brand of ugliness. As Meredith said:

"Behold the life of ease, it drifts,
   The chastened life commands its course.
She winnows, winnows roughly, sifts,
   To dip her chosen in her source,
   Contention is the vital force,
When pluck they brains, her prize of gifts."

[186]

The struggle for existence, as Darwin pointed out so carefully, means much more than a life-and-death competition around the platter of subsistence. Its color is not always red. It includes all the efforts that living creatures make against environing difficulties and limitations, and it rises to an endeavor after well-being that man himself might usefully admire. We must avoid the caricature of organic nature which depicts it as "a vast gladiatorial show," a "dismal cockpit"; for although there is competition to the death and no lack of rapid bloodshed, there is much more than this in the struggle for existence. It includes the industry of the long-tailed tit in gathering 2,379 feathers to furnish a life-saving quilt for the eggs and young ones in the nest. To speak of Nature "red in tooth and claw with rapine" is no doubt to emphasize one aspect of the struggle for existence, but another aspect is illustrated even by such patterns of carnivorousness as the otter and the ermine, who devote much time and care to educating their offspring in all the ways of the woods. One poet tells us how the hedgerow shrieks with blood, and another tells us that no animal is unhappy over all the others. Both statements are extreme; it is necessary to recognize the co-existence of individualistic and coöperative ways of living, of self-assertion and self-subordination, flourishing cheek by jowl. More important, however, than the precise mode of the struggle for existence is the general fact that Nature's method, so far as we understand it, implies an endless sifting.

All through the ages there has been an elimination of those with the unlit lamp or the ungirt loin. Nature's first voice is—Struggle, Endeavor, Struggle. A lion's skin is never cheap. What is worth gaining and what is worth keeping must be fought for. One of the obvious lessons of organic evolution is the danger of having things made too easy. What would our hereditary character have been without Nature's millennial sifting out of the sluggish, the dull, the feckless, the unbalanced, the unhealthy? What would our hereditary character have been without Nature's millennial approbation of the insurgent, the adventurous, the controlled, the far-sighted, the strenuous—meaning by approbation the award of survival and success? No doubt the tapeworm in its inglorious life of ease is a product of evolution as well as the golden eagle in its fast-nesses, but there is no denying that the better places in life have been accorded to the more finely strung

[188]

creatures, such as birds and mammals. Nature's chief rewards have gone to those types that coveted the best gifts. In any case it is a scientific fact that

> "Life is not as idle ore,
> But iron dug from central gloom,
> And heated hot with burning fears,
> And dipt in baths of hissing tears,
> And battered by the shocks of doom
> To shape and use."

One of the greatest difficulties of modern life is due to man's necessary attempt to get out of hearing of Nature's first voice, which bids him struggle. In early days mankind was much in the scene of natural selection—the meshes being wild beasts, changes of climate, pitiless forces of Nature, scarcity of food, unchecked microbes, and so on, and we are today the better for this long winnowing. But man gradually strengthened his foothold and rose higher and higher in his masterfulness. As everyone knows, the whole trend of human evolution since civilization began has been to throw off the yoke of natural selection. Some of its thraldom remains, as in cases of differential death rate, where the inherently weaker succumb in larger numbers, but we are continually interfering necessarily and rightly—with the sifting operations of disease, hard times, and the like. This interference has been largely ethical, for there has been a growth of kindly feeling and an increased sense of social solidarity. We cannot but hold out the helping hand. Furthermore, the development of social organization must in itself automatically tend to shield and shelter individual types that would be eliminated forthwith if there were no society. This is seen even among the ants, where so-called master species, unable to fend for themselves, are fed by their slaves! So human society tends to shelter the physically unfit. No one can forget that weaklings have often shaken the world, or that Sir Isaac Newton began as a very miserable infant, yet on the whole there is a danger in relaxed sifting. This is what Herbert Spencer called "the dilemma of civilization": "Any arrangements which, in a considerable degree, prevent superiority from profiting by the rewards of superiority, or shield inferiority from the evils it entails—any arrangements which make it as well to be inferior as to be superior, are arrangements diametrically opposed to the progress of organization, and the reaching of a higher life." There is no single remedy; we can but try to substitute higher for lower modes of struggle, and avoid everything that favors the multiplication of the obviously undesirable. We cannot any longer tolerate Nature's régime; we must heal the sick, save the children, and prevent the wastage of life, but there is no gainsaying the danger of being so kind in the present that we are cruel to the future. We must criticize the modes of sifting that are in operation in our midst, and seek to improve them as factors in all-round evolution.

The second voice of Nature that the Hebrew prophet heard was the earthquake—a symbol, we take it, of the emotional voice, for is there anything so awful that stirs man and beast more deeply, that moves us down to the primeval bed-rock of human nature laid down in the time of the cave-dwellers? This second voice says: "Be still; be reverent; wonder; enjoy." As Aristotle said, there is throughout Nature something of the astounding, and the sense of wonder is one of the saving graces of life. It has often promoted science; it has often led to the footstool of religion. Sometimes it is an overflowing enjoyment of the beautiful; sometimes it is an overwhelming sense of the awesome. It may be in the star-strewn sky, or in the mystery of the mountains, or in the sea eternally new, or in the way of the eagle in the air, or in the look in a dog's eyes, or in the tinkling of the bluebells by the wayside; but somewhere there should be an experience which we confess to be too wonderful for us. No doubt the object of wonder changes from age to age, and even with our years. In our childhood we wondered greatly at the sunbeam dancing on the walls and roof of the darkened room where we lay resting; and it was long before we discovered that it was due to the reflection from the tossing polished leaves of the evergreens outside the window. We have ceased to wonder at the sunbeam, but have we learned to wonder enough at the light itself? The poet Keats said that he could not forgive Newton for dissolving the mystery of the rainbow, but was not Wordsworth wiser in discerning that when science removes a minor wonder it leaves a larger wonder in our ken? "My heart leaps up when I behold a rainbow in the sky. So was it when I was a child; So be it when I shall grow old; or let me die." Science dissipates clouds and leaves blue sky. Behind each wonder there is another deeper or higher, till we come to the fundamental mysteriousness of the irreducibles—protons and electrons; elec-

tro-magnetic vibrations or ether waves; and the mind
that measures all. And when we strain at the end
of our scientific reach, there rise the questions that
send tendrils *beyond science*. Whence came all;
whither goeth all; and what is the purpose of it all?
For science, as such, knows nothing and asks nothing
in regard to *the* beginning or *the* ending, or *the*
meaning behind the long process. Science *describes
and formulates* in terms of the lowest common de-
nominators available; religion seeks to interpret in
terms of the greatest common measure. "In the
beginning was mind."

> "Nay what is nature's self
> But an endless
> Strife towards music,
> Euphony, rhyme?
>
> "Trees in their blooming,
> Tides in their flowing,
> Stars in their circling,
> Tremble with song.
>
> "God on His throne is
> Eldest of Poets,
> Unto His measures
> Moveth the whole."

No doubt science dissipates the minor wonders, but there is usually some relapse into commonplaceness if the fairy gold for one generation becomes only withered leaves for the next. To the thoughtful botanist the Dryad is still in the free, though it cannot of course have a diagram in his text-book. Though science as such is entirely unemotional and must keep feeling at a spear's length, yet to the synoptic vision science does not cease to contribute the illuminating rays that excite wonder. Emerson had the right idea of wonder behind wonder when he pictured the boy looking through the maple branches at the moon and the stars:

"Over his head were the maple buds,
    And over the tree was the moon:
And over the moon were the starry studs
    That drop from the angels' shoon."

When the half-wonders go, the major wonders come. When the half-gods go, the God arrives. As Meredith discerned, "You of any well that springs may unfold the heaven of things."

Although a sense of the wonder, the mysterious, the awesome is, we think, peculiarly associated with religious, poetic, and artistic emotion, it is also of human value in arousing curiosity and in stimulating interest. Every cloud is a challenge to science, prompting inquiry. Every wonder is an added interest to life. When we cease to wonder, we are beginning to die. "It is enough that through Thy grace, I've seen nought common on Thy earth. Take not that vision from my ken." As we begin to become more at home in Nature, our wonder rises into what may almost be called affection. This is the reward of those who have what Meredith called a "love exceeding a simple love of the things that glide in grasses and rubble of woody wreck." It was one whose life was far from being all roses who said:

"To make this earth our hermitage,
A cheerful and a changeful page
God's bright and intricate device
Of days and seasons doth suffice."

Apart from even higher ambitions, it is a noble one to desire to see more and more of the goodness of God in the land of the living, and to make each day more and more a satisfaction in itself. This is a deep piety, and it is helped by a cultivation of the sense of wonder. "Praised be the fathomless universe," said Walt Whitman, "for life and joy, *for objects and knowledge* curious." It was an epiphany that he saw:

(1) "I believe a leaf of grass is no less than the journey work of the stars;
(2) And the pismire is equally perfect and the grain of sand and the egg of the wren;
(3) The running bramble would adorn the parlours of heaven, and the tree-toad is a masterpiece for the highest.
(4) The narrowest hinge in my hand puts to scorn all machinery;
(5) The cow crunching with depressed head surpasses any statue;
    And a mouse is enough to stagger sextillions of infidels."

There is no difficulty in finding a modern basis for reasonable wonder. We may find it in the abundance of power in the world, in the immensities of the cosmos, in the intricacy of the pattern woven out of three or four kinds of thread, in the orderliness of nature, in the omnipresent beauty, in the insurgence of life, and in the expanding reality of progressive evolution.

One likes the story of the old sailorman who had seen all the wonders of the deep for forty years, and all the wonders of the world around the seven seas, but when they asked him what in all his life had impressed him most, he answered, "The nails on a baby's fingers." He had a cultivated sense of wonder, for the wonderful is not the colossal or the stupendous or the startling, but that which gives us most suggestion of meaning and pervading significance.

Even better is the story of the visitor from a Midland town who could not tear himself away from the window in Regent Street, London, where the makers of incubators show the chicks scrambling out of the eggs. This is a familiar sight to those who have been brought up in the country, but it is almost startling to those who see it for the first time. As his two friends insisted on going on, the delighted observer turned to continue his sight-seeing, and was heard to say, "Now *that's* a thing to have seen; after *that* there beant no use their telling me that there be no God."

Perhaps we cannot get beyond what Coleridge said so wisely: "All knowledge begins and ends with wonder, but the first wonder is the child of ignorance, while the second is the parent of adoration." Nature's second voice is that which bids us make it part of the serious business of our life to try to replace the first wonder by the second.

The third voice of Nature that the Hebrew prophet heard was the *fire;* and we take this to be the symbol of the scientific voice, which says Inquire. For the fire of science burns up superstitious rubbish, melts out the fine gold of accurate knowledge, reduces things to a common denominator, and gives light to man.

From the first, when man was able to look out with clear eyes, Nature has been setting him problems, prompting his inquisitiveness, leading him gradually from the practical to the more abstract. Lafcadio Hearn tells us that in the house of any old Japanese family the guest is likely to be shown some of the heirlooms. "A pretty little box, perhaps, will be set before you. Opening it, you will see only a beautiful silk bag, closed with a silk running-cord decked with tiny tassels. . . . You open the bag and see within it another bag of a different quality of silk, but very fine. Open that, and, lo! a third, which contains a fourth, which contains a fifth, which contains a sixth, which contains a seventh bag, which contains the strongest, roughest, hardest vessel of Chinese clay that you ever beheld; yet it is not only curious but precious; it may be more than a thousand years old." Indeed, it is more than clay; there is an idea in it.

Now natural science has to do with a similar process of unwrapping—it opens the beautiful box, it removes one silken envelope after another, trying at the same time to unravel the pattern and count the threads—and what is finally revealed is something very old and wonderful—the stuff out of which worlds have been spun—"a handful of dust which God enchants." For there seems to be high wisdom in trying to see the scientific denominator in the light of the philosophic greatest common measure.

Varying the metaphor, one of the foremost discoverers of new knowledge, Sir J. J. Thomson, writes: "As we conquer peak after peak we see in front of us regions full of interest and beauty, but we do not see our goal, we do not see the horizon; in the distance tower still higher peaks, which will yield to those who ascend them still wider prospects, and deepen the feeling, the truth of which is emphasized by every advance in science, that 'Great are the words of the Lord.' Science is like an asymptotic curve always drawing nearer to a goal, but never reaching it."

It is the wonderful achievement of modern science to have reduced all the forms of matter to groups of electrons and protons, and to have brought all the radiant energies into line as ether-waves or electro-magnetic vibrations.

These are the physical irreducibles, and whenever we think of living creatures, we must add another, namely *mind*. For by no jugglery can we get mind out of electricity and ether, with which it is incommensurable. One of the reasons why we should listen to the third voice of nature, which says so insistently, *Search, Inquire,* is that we thereby come to a better understanding of man's place in the *systema naturae,* and to a better understanding of the partial or abstract character of science. For it clears our way when we understand that science is not the whole of knowledge, but simply the kind that we get by following precise methods of observation and experiment. It may be compared to fishing in the sea with nets of a particular kind of mesh. It is an assumption that there is no kind of knowledge save that which this kind of net will catch. If we are fully to know our native land, we must appreciate its beauty as well as its geology, but we do not appreciate its beauty by scientific methods. No one supposes that his knowledge of his mother depends wholly on what he has discovered in regard to her heredity and the like; why should anyone suppose that man's knowledge of his *alma mater* must be wholly based on science? Our point is that there are other rights of way toward truth besides the rugged pathway of science. Nature's third voice, *Inquire,* does not restrict us to scientific methods; we may also learn in the sanctuary of feeling and along the pathway of obedience. *Vivendo discimus.*

But the third voice, *Inquire,* has another value besides clearing the eyes of our understanding, it tells man how to enter more and more fully into his kingdom. As Bacon said: "Knowledge is not only for the glory of the Creator, but for the relief of man's estate. And not for the relief only, but for its extension and enhancement." How many of the great advances in modern civilization, shadowed as some have been, are due to man's obedience to the voice that bids him face the facts? As Spencer said, "Life is not for science, so much as science is for life." As Comte said, "Knowledge is foresight, and foresight is power." One of the lessons that man

[201]

is learning, quickly now in some directions, slowly, however, in others, is the duty of Inquiry. When he is in difficulties he must search; when he would extend his kingdom he must take science as his torch. In order to control, we must first understand.

It seems to us that the three great voices of Nature are Endeavor, Enjoy, and Inquire; or, at another pitch, Struggle, Revere, Search. No one can tell how far man may go by listening to and obeying these three voices; but it has been a common experience of mankind that a limit comes to practical endeavor, to emotional intensity, and to resolute thinking. But it is characteristic of man to insist on pressing beyond these limits; and activities at the strain-limits have often taken the form of religion. Man has done all he can, and is baffled, therefore he has often prayed. Man's cup of joy or of sorrow has overflowed, and he has often found relief in psalm and lament, in song and sacrifice. Man has often reached for the time being the limit of his understanding, yet the questions *whence, whither,* and *why* clamor for answer; and what can he do but make the adventure of faith? Thus from listening to the three voices of Nature, symbolized somewhat loudly by wind, earthquake, and fire, man has many

[202]

a time heard in the quietness of his heart the voice of God. Perhaps what the prophet heard was not so much a "still small voice" as the voice that is heard when all is quiet. It had seemed to him, as he listened to the wind, the earthquake, and the fire, that God was not in any of them; but one cannot help thinking that in *obeying* the voice heard in the quietness he came to understand afterward that God had been in the other experiences as well.

In any case, if we can pass from the cold evening light of science, which the schoolmen called *cognitio vespertina,* to the morning light of religion, which they called *cognitio matutina,* we may be able to agree more and more with Ruskin's fine words (engraved on the memorial at Derwentwater): "The Spirit of God is around you in the air that you breathe, His glory in the light that you see, and in the fruitfulness of the earth and the joy of its creatures. He has written for you day by day His revelation, and He has granted you day by day your daily bread."

MORALS AND HEALTH

by Sir Thomas Horder

Morals and Health

By Sir Thomas Horder

IF I were a preacher I should talk to the people collected together in much the same way as I hope I talk to them individually when they seek my advice. I do not think I ought to talk to them in any other way, and I should try to resist the temptation—which the idea of one sermon only in a lifetime would tend to induce—to propound a theory of life, and fit facts into it as nicely as is possible. A doctor's life gives little enough time for the contemplation which is demanded in order to found a philosophy of his own, nor does his experience fit him very well to be a good disciple of the philosophies of others. But it should be possible to weave into a message to the general public the innumerable little individual messages of which the doctor delivers himself daily in the consulting-room and at the bedside. Anyway, I have decided to make the attempt.

Since the idea underlying a sermon is a moral one,

this attempt presupposes that I consider much of the doctor's life-work, and much of the advice he gives, to have a moral aspect. That is so, and it is that conviction which makes this sermon possible. I believe firmly that the basis of the relations between the doctor and the sick man is made up of that same set of principles which have been known to govern life and conduct since human society first began. Superficial thinkers sometimes object that medicine is a conservative science: they are generally led to this idea by finding that the moral code which influenced Hippocrates two thousand years ago influences his disciples today. But it is the assurance that this same moral code still operates which makes it easy for the patient to come and unload his burden of sickness, both bodily and mental, and thus take the first step toward health.

Of the doctor's equipment for dealing with the problem it were invidious to say much. There is that subtle but paramount thing termed personality. There are patience and sympathy. The rest of the outfit is contributed by science and a mind trained in detecting essentials and disregarding non-essentials. Personality without science makes the doctor a quack, and science without personality leads to the medicine of the academy, not of the sick-room.

PRIMARY VIRTUES

Most, if not all, of the primary virtues come, sooner or later, into the relations of patient and doctor. It is essential that both parties should cultivate them if health is to be restored and established. Honesty of purpose is obligatory. The cultivation of mutual confidence is not less so. Patience, not only in itself a virtue, but mother of many virtues, must go hand-in-hand with persistent endeavor. Courage, too, is imperative, for the chief enemy, and generally the one last to be overcome, is fear. Panic dissipates effort and abolishes morale, and both of these things must be jealously conserved.

Upon this stock of virtues science must be grafted. Not the science of any school merely, but science that is limitless; knowledge gained from all ages and, if need be, from every quarter of the universe. All must be swept up and transmuted into appropriate remedies for the treatment of the sick man. No doctrine or sect must cramp the means of healing and no name, however great, must alone dictate the way of salvation. To have recourse to science of such sort is a sacred obligation laid upon every doctor.

Nor should he despair because of the many and varied excursions into empiricism which, through ignorance and credulity, the harassed patient often makes. Science, that quiet but efficient servant of mankind, will, in the long run, shame all the noisy promises of the untrained hireling. If there is nothing much amiss, and very little at stake, a gamble in pseudo-science, or in obscurantism, tickles his mind and enables the patient to enjoy a tilt at orthodoxy. But in the serious affairs of life it is the expert who scores the success, and, in the end, wisdom is found to be justified of her children. The anti-mind is a disease that finds its own physic and in its own way. It is only when it begins to proselytize that it becomes a nuisance to society.

THE DOCTOR'S FUNCTION

What, now, is the doctor's aim? Is it to achieve equilibrium, for this is health, be it the body or the mind, or both, that demand his help. And his attention must be fixed upon both of these factors, seeing that the association between them is so close. He wages war against premature death, against disability, and against pain—all of them evil things—and no quarter is to be given. But again and again he fails? It is true. Failure from lack of wisdom reflects upon himself; failure from lack of available knowledge does not. Our power over disease grows, but grows all too slowly. Some defects there are that seem almost hopeless of cure, even with the growth of science: defects of heredity, congenital diseases, faults of the mind. But who shall limit the bounds of science?

Nor do we employ all the help that science, even now, offers to us. There exist many means of cure, and still more means of prevention of disease, which ignorance and prejudice render inoperative. As for advancing science, we spend vast sums of money upon wasteful and destructive issues, a fraction of which might well speed up research, so that a goodly number of diseases, so-called incurable, would no longer deserve this epithet. We make war, tolerate slums, encourage vices and disease-producing luxuries, yet we decry the gaps in knowledge whereby our bodies and souls remain sick.

It is necessary to strike a deeper note, and to speak

of the doctor's function in relation to the more complex issues of life. We are a strangely differing set of persons in his eyes when we are viewed as prospective patients. At one end of the scale a few of us are Nature's darlings: we can scarcely be ill, either in mind or body, even though we try. At the other end are a larger group of us who find it very difficult to be anything else than ill. Some of us in this group start life with heavy handicaps. Our very temperaments are ofttimes a menace to us. Or our complexions or stature speak of hidden tendencies to disease that we may never entirely escape. Or there may lurk in the blood and other tissues the seeds of maladies that wait to strike us down after a few years of joyous health. Or we may even start the race misshapen, and with a necessary part of our equipment absent or defective. A veritable martyrdom awaits some of us, so that the "health and a day" by which we may "make the pomp of emperors ridiculous" sounds like a cruel jibe.

LIFE AN ART

Between these two extremes come the great majority of us; we start with good health and, having run the gauntlet of our children's ills successfully, we can remain healthy if we will, so long as the accident of disease does not overtake us in permanently disabling fashion. Healthy or unhealthy we must be, since there is, in all of us, a vital force which provides the momentum to go on, and to achieve. Æons ago this aim was primitive—food, warmth, protection from the enemy, and desire for the mate. Then, slowly through the ages, emerged æsthetics and the moral law, and life at last became an art. To attain distinction in conduct a healthy body and a healthy mind, though perhaps not essential, are of the utmost help. To keep them, therefore, is one of our foremost duties.

This preservation of health does not depend upon the meticulous observance of a set of inhibitions, whether in food or in other things. It depends upon temperance and a quiet mind. To live long depends chiefly upon our forebears; to live healthily depends chiefly upon ourselves. More important than the food we eat is the degree in which we succeed in disciplining ourselves and the habits that we form. Self-discipline none of us can escape if a heritage of good health is to be ours for life; and certainly we cannot escape this salutary check upon the tendency

[213]

which is present in all of us to drift, if we desire that fuller heritage of becoming, in our character, a little lower than the angels.

HEAVEN'S FIRST LAW

If circumstances have not enjoined some exigency in our lives, we must perforce introduce it ourselves. Such creatures of habit are we that it is only thus that the body and the mind can alike be kept taut. Some routine is as essential to health and to happiness as is some relaxation. If order is heaven's first law, earth cannot hope to escape the same necessity.

The cultivation of a quiet mind—equanimity—is imperative in the maintenance of health. Jesus taught a fundamental lesson in mental hygiene when he bade us live one day at a time. The man who brings forward tomorrow's anticipated troubles, and carries over yesterday's useless regrets, so overloads today's duties that he is already sick at heart when the sun rises.

As for the great mysteries that face us all, the whence and the whither of life, it is a good thing to find that the solution of these questions is not necessary for service or (let us hope) for salvation. Efforts at conceiving the absolute make the brain reel, but within the relative and the limited there is ample scope for conduct, though a few of us may prefer to spend our lives in efforts at contemplating the infinite. The Golden Rule still serves us as a sufficient guide, and would appear to be above creeds and even independent of our ultimate destiny.

A FUNDAMENTAL FACTOR

Faced as he is with law, with progress, with development, the doctor has a quiet confidence in the things he cannot see and in the future that he does not know. Far from being a materialist, as is often supposed, his faith is a fundamental factor in his work. For him the process of the suns is right and secure, though he might well say, at times, with Job, "How small a whisper do we hear of him." He is more "spiritual" than many to whom this epithet is given, for he believes firmly that heaven is with us now, whenever we obey the laws of cause and effect, "the chancellors of God," be it in the realm of the body or of the soul.

He is a little impatient with those who view this life as a mere ante-chamber to a life to come: this life's duties are so obvious and our contribution to "that far-off divine event" is so intimately bound up with the manner in which we perform them. His own duty is very clear: he must interpret the law to his patients, and he must make it clear to them exactly wherein they have broken it. In as true a sense as was the case with Paul he should be able to say, "Whom ye ignorantly worship, him declare I unto you."

And so I reiterate the belief with which I began. The art of healing is based upon deep-seated law, and it is impossible to separate the moral from the physical law. To break either leads to disease or pain, and recovery or relief can only be achieved by a renewal of obedience and loyalty. And the means by which this may be done?

Gentleness, Virtue, Wisdom, and Endurance,
These are the seals of that most firm assurance
    Which bars the pit over Destruction's strength . . .
These are the spells by which to reassume
An Empire o'er the disentangled doom.

ON THE EVILS DUE TO FEAR
by Hon. Bertrand Russell

On the Evils Due to Fear

By Hon. Bertrand Russell

IF I were about to be executed and were allowed twenty minutes in which to make a farewell address, what should I say? It would be necessary to be brief and simple, and I think I should concentrate upon one issue, namely the importance of eliminating fear. I do not imagine that mankind can be made perfect; whatever may be done, some defects will survive, but a great many of the defects from which adults suffer are due to preventable mistakes in their education, and the most important of these mistakes is the inculcation of fear. Parents, priests, and governments have despaired of maintaining their authority by an appeal to reason, and have preferred to produce abject, cowering slaves. I do not believe that any good thing is to be obtained through fear, and I hold that obedience not otherwise obtainable had better not be obtained. The objections to fear as a social force are of two kinds.

There are the bad effects upon those who cause terror, and the bad effects upon those who suffer it. Both are grave, though the latter more so.

To begin with those who inspire terror. They inevitably become cruel and fond of thwarting others; they grow impatient of opposition and argument, and of every kind of reasoning tending to show that they have misused their authority. They come to prefer persons without self-respect and without principle. They are themselves inevitably filled with fears. They fear to lose their unjust authority; they fear to rouse merited resentment in their underlings; they fear that the world may become more reasonable. These fears lead them to increase their cruelty, and every increase of cruelty increases their fear of reprisals. Thus there is a vicious circle tending to a perpetual intensification of the connected evils of tyranny and apprehension.

The effects of fear upon those who feel it are, however, very much worse. There are various kinds of fear; of these, physical fear, which alone is traditionally despised, is by far the least harmful. Moral and intellectual fears are far worse. All fear inspires a greater or less degree of rage, which, since it dare not vent itself upon the dreaded object, finds

[220]

an outlet in tyranny over whatever is weaker. Just as in the holders of power cruelty begets fear, so in their slaves fear begets cruelty. Fear of social disapproval is probably one of the chief causes of meanness and unkindness in the modern world. People enjoy expressing social disapproval because they themselves have been thwarted by the fear of incurring it. When a man has sacrificed something of importance in order to retain the good opinion of his neighbors, he is naturally furious when some one else refuses to make the sacrifice, and he therefore becomes a fierce moralist, determined to punish the bold sinner. The sinners punished by social disapproval include almost all who are not hypocrites, all who have new ideas of a not purely scientific kind, and all who practice any morality more generous or less vindictive than that of their own herd. Fear of social disapproval is, therefore, a very dangerous quality to inculcate. Social coöperation should be voluntary and reasonable, not a craven submission of each to all.

One of the worst effects of fear is that it produces stupidity. Intelligence requires a certain kind of intellectual fearlessness; it requires, at any rate, a capacity for intellectual independence, and intellectual independence will hardly be found where there is no degree of social independence. For this reason, societies which prize social cohesion unduly are almost sure to be composed of stupid individuals. They will, therefore, become incapable of progress, either scientifically or socially. Not even the most ardent feminist can deny that women have shown much less intellectual independence than men. I believe this to be mainly due to the fact that they have been more rigidly subjugated than men to a morality of fear. The recognized method of producing virtue in women has been the fear of social ostracism on earth, and hell fire hereafter. In order that these fears may acquire a firm hold, girls have been taught, from their earliest years, to be timid in their thoughts and to avoid following any argument to its logical conclusion, on the ground that all logical conclusions are unladylike. They have thus been left to practice the vices of the coward— envy, backbiting, and petty-mindedness. What the traditional moralist apparently fails to recognize is that the mental attitude leading to such vice causes infinitely more misery than a more fearless attitude which might sometimes lead to generous sins, but would never lead to ungenerous vices.

I regard with horror all those whose business is to keep the human spirit and the human intellect in fetters. I include among these almost all ministers of religion, a large proportion of school teachers, 90 per cent. of magistrates and judges, and a large proportion of those who have earned the respect of the community by their insistence on what is called a rigid moral standard. These different classes of men are all engaged in their several ways in endeavoring by means of social disapproval, or the criminal law, to produce belief in propositions which every candid inquirer can see to be at best doubtful, and which every student of statistics knows to be socially harmful. Take for example, the following facts from an American official publication: out of every thousand children born in America the number who die during the first year is: among the Portuguese 200.3, among the French-Canadians 171.3, among the Poles 157.2, among the native white population 93.8, and among the Jews 53.5. These figures show clearly that the infant mortality is proportional to the intensity of belief in the Christian religion. Herod caused nothing like such a massacre of innocents as is caused by Catholic dogma, and one of my reasons for publicly com-

[223]

bating what I regard as superstition is to prevent this needless suffering of helpless children. And the harm done by Christianity is very largely due to the fact that it has its psychological roots in fear.

When I say that fear is an evil, I do not mean that it can be adequately combated by conscious courage. Conscious courage does not eliminate fear, it merely prevents people from acting upon it; it thus involves a state of nervous tension which is almost sure to produce disastrous results. The right methods for avoiding fear depend upon the kind of fear involved. There are in the first place purely imaginary fears; such, for example, is the fear that eating ham or practicing birth control will be punished by an angry Deity. Such fears are instilled in youth with a view to producing certain kinds of conduct; they can be combated very simply by merely omitting to teach belief in false propositions to the young.ⱼ I know it will be said that the young will not be virtuous unless they believe false propositions. This is a most curious attitude resting upon a twofold fallacy. There is first the belief that virtuous behavior is something in favor of which no rational argument can be given, and second the further belief that irrational and untrue arguments are going to be sufficient to lead to painful self-denials, which admittedly cannot be defended on any reasonable ground. To teach rational behavior is undoubtedly difficult, but it is certainly easier by rational than by irrational means. Accustom a child to suppose that there are good reasons for what you say; let him verify for himself that this is the case wherever such verification is possible to him. Tell him nothing whatsoever that you do not seriously believe to be true. Cultivate his scientific spirit, so that he will for himself test your assertions when he can, and you will produce in the end a human being capable of a degree of rationality entirely impossible to those who have been brought up upon a conception of sin derived from arbitrary theological prohibitions. If it be said that rational human beings will not conform to the whole of the ethical code that has been inculcated by the Church, so much the worse for that code.

There is another class of fears where danger is real but can be eliminated by sufficient skill. The simplest examples of this are physical dangers such as are incurred in mountain-climbing. But there are a large number of others. Take, for example, the danger of social disapproval. It is quite true that one man may steal a horse while another man may not look over the hedge; this difference depends mainly upon a certain kind of difference in instinctive attitude toward other people. The man who expects to be ill-treated will be, while the man who approaches his fellows in fearless friendliness will find this attitude justified by results. Boys who are afraid of dogs run away from them, which causes the dogs to come yapping at their heels, while boys who like dogs find that the dogs like them. Exactly the same thing applies to our behavior in regard to other people, but the right result cannot be produced by screwing up one's courage to face what one believes to be hostility; it can be produced only by a certain genuine friendliness and expectation of friendliness.

There is yet a third class of dangers which cannot altogether be avoided, but which may be felt to be more or less terrible according to a man's outlook. Such, for example, is the danger of financial loss. A great part of many people's lives is overshadowed by the fear of poverty. Great poverty such as that of a wage-earner out of work is undoubtedly a very terrible evil, but the comparative poverty which well-to-do business men dread is only rendered a serious evil by misdirection of interests and tastes. The reasons for desiring wealth are luxury and ostentation. Luxury is the pleasure of lazy men who do not enjoy any form of activity, and ostentation is the pleasure of those whose principal desire is to be envied by fools. Neither of these pleasures will be strong in those whose active impulses have been allowed free play in youth, but a discipline based upon fear too often curbs these impulses, since virtuous parents fear that they will lead to sin, and fussy parents fear that they will lead to danger. Almost all sound education consists in providing opportunities for activities. An undesirable form of activity should not be directly checked, but should be replaced by creating an environment in which some more useful form becomes more attractive. The result will be the production of human beings who do not desire great wealth, and do not greatly fear its loss if they happen to acquire it. Fear of social disapproval should be met in the same way, not by teaching people to resist heroically the impulses to conformity, but by teaching them a certain kind of self-respect which will make them comparatively indifferent to the approval of the herd, so long as they have the approval of their own judgment and of those whose opinion is worthy of respect.

I do not wish to suggest that absence of fear is alone enough to produce a good human being; undoubtedly other things are necessary. But I do suggest that freedom from fear is *one* of the most important things to aim at, and is perhaps more easily achieved by a wise education than any other equally desirable quality. Freedom from fear confers physical, moral, and intellectual benefits. Miss Margaret McMillan points out that children who are frequently scolded do not breathe rightly, and are thus more apt than other children to suffer from adenoids. Many other examples could be given of the way in which fear damages health, more especially through its interference with digestion. The moral damage that it does is even more important. This damage is partly a result of the injury to health, for, as is now well known, many of the gravest moral defects are connected with bad functioning of the digestive processes. Of this, avarice is a notable example. But the most important evil due to fear is the attitude of rage against the world. Dr. John B. Watson has demonstrated that the instinctive stimulus to rage in new-born infants is constriction of the limbs, or anything that interferes with freedom of movement. From this origin, through the process of conditioned reflexes studied by Pavlov, the rage reaction grows out gradually, so that it comes to be elicited by a number of other stimuli. When a man fears his fellows, he reacts in defense as he would react if they were actually interfering with his liberty of movement. At least he reacts in this way so far as his emotions are concerned, but the overt expression of rage is partly inhibited by his fears, and therefore he looks about unconsciously for some safe outlet. He may find this in religious or moral persecution, in love of war, in opposition to humanitarian innovations, in oppression of his children, or in all of these combined. All these vices are in nine cases out of ten a result of hidden fears.

Intellectually, also, fear has disastrous results. There is the fear of any unusual opinion which prevents men from thinking straight on any subject on which their neighbors have foolish opinions. Then there is the fear of death, which prevents men from thinking straight on theological subjects; and then there is the fear of self-direction, which leads men to seek some authority to which they can submit their judgment. These various forms of fear are

[229]

responsible for quite half the stupidity in the world. Most of the stock of fear with which men and women go through life is implanted in them during the first six years of childhood, either with a view to making them "good" or by contagion from the fears of parents. For my part, I care nothing for the virtue which is rooted in fear, and I should seek everywhere, but more especially in early education, to produce human beings capable of social coöperation to the necessary extent for reasons with which fear should have nothing whatever to do. This is in my opinion the essential problem of moral education—a problem by no means insoluble, and only thought to be difficult owing to the weight of prejudice and cruel tradition.

THE ROAD TO REDEMPTION
by Dr. Joseph Collins

The Road to Redemption

By Dr. Joseph Collins

"Behold I was shapen in iniquity and
in sin did my mother conceive me."
—PSALM li:5.

MY SERMON shall be a discussion of a subject to
which I have devoted forty years of unremitting toil
—*viz.,* the redemption of man. Redemption of his
body, to be sure, but that he might accomplish the
purpose for which he was created—self-realization.

I am convinced that he who accomplishes that is
far more likely to save his soul than he who fails
to do it.

Retrospectively, I see that my struggle has been
with two foes: sin and ignorance, the parents of
fear. Fear is universal. Everyone is afraid of something: of pain and disease, of defalcation and defeat,
of reality and unreality, of death, and of life. One
fears for his soul, another for his body, a third for
his goods. We admit and realize the potency of

fear as enemy of health and happiness, but we make little effort to discover and destroy its source. He who will purge man of fear will stem the tide of impotence and misery as Pasteur stemmed the tide of disease a generation ago.

Those who have devoted themselves to prying into nature's secrets during the last forty years have been successful beyond the most optimistic imagination. Ignorance is being dispelled so rapidly that we are breathless merely contemplating it. When we shall have made as much progress with man as we have with the world, we shall reflect enlightenment as shimmering water reflects moonlight. There is no encouragement from the past that we shall make any headway with sin. We wallow in it now as we did a year ago, a thousand years ago. It not only fetters our feet, manacles our hands, stupefies our intellect, anæsthetizes our emotions, but it engenders, develops, and matures fear, man's mortal enemy.

The behaviorist school of psychology contends that fear is engendered in infants chiefly by loud noises and sudden withdrawal of support. It may be so, but the origin of the fears I have encountered have been predominantly in the doctrine of sin, its origin and transmission, its eventuation and penalties. Sin is man made. Its purpose is to make him conform to a certain code of ethics, framed by those who claimed they were inspired and by others who arrogate to themselves peculiar knowledge of God's designs. They sought and still seek to make man indulge his instincts in accordance with rules which they make. The penalty for breaking these rules is eternal punishment which, until recently, it was universally taught was imposed in a place called hell.

Fear of death that may entail eternal torment is one of the commonest fears of youth. Fear of God is said to be the beginning of wisdom, but why one should fear Him who is all compassion, tenderness, forbearance, clemency, and mercy is beyond understanding. We do not fear those to whom we owe our being, our birth, our weal; we love, revere, worship them and we do everything we can to testify our affection and obligation.

Until we have a different conception of God, and a new attitude toward Him (which is the essence of religion, indeed is religion), fear will continue to gnaw and devour us, and we shall make small headway in overcoming and eradicating it until we forget or modify the current doctrine of sin. There is small chance that it can be accomplished. Fear prevents us from undertaking it, even from contemplating it.

What is sin? No one knows, yet everyone feels that he knows. There is no agreement between theologians, ethicians, and philosophers as to the definition of sin. Theologians themselves are not in accord, nor are the other two groups, for that matter. Some identify sin with deviation from the Christian standard of perfection; some restrict it to intentional breaches of moral law; others include as sins conscious, even deliberate, procedures, such as satisfaction of healthy appetites, yielding to instinctive reaction.

For the ethician, sin is a moral evil, anything infracting the standards of "right" and "good," the ideal of the latter being the life and teaching of Christ. Anything which misses this mark is sin, whether the subject of the deficiency is accountable or not.

The theological conception of sin is not exclusively an ethical conception; it is a voluntary transgression of the law of God, an attitude or activity that contravenes a law which the agent does or can recognize as binding upon himself. Sin is thus a

[236]

moral imperfection for which the agent is in God's sight accountable. Roman Catholics include in the law of God all commandments that emanate from legitimate authority and consequently ecclesiastic laws, civil laws, and the just precepts of parents and superiors. They take refuge behind the statement, "He that resisteth the power, resisteth the ordinance of God," and they differentiate between sin and vice; the former is an act, the latter a habit. Sin, for them, is both original and personal. The former is annihilated by baptism, the latter by contrition, confession, and penance.

For me, there is but one sin—cruelty; hurting for the pleasure of giving pain, whether it be with blow or word; but there are many crimes. It is the duty of the state to deal with the latter; that of the individual to combat and destroy the former. Were I a prophet, I should say that kindliness to all domestic creation is a passport to paradise.

Sin, for the originator of Christianity, was a "transgression of the law," culpability in act or thought, and the law was to love God and love man. Any attachment which interfered with wholehearted devotion to God was sinful, and especially devotion to goods or mammon. Inhumanity, hypocrisy, moral barrenness and rejection of the mercy and love of God are the sins that cause most complete estrangement from God; yet these are the sins that are committed every day by practically everyone. What greater proof of our inhumanity could be had than the slums of every large city? Is it not devotion to goods and mammon for a Church to have assets of upward of fourteen millions of dollars, thirteen of which is in productive real estate? How can such possession be reconciled with the teachings of Christ? Is it not the most crass hypocrisy to spend millions of dollars in the construction of cathedrals and of temples wherein to worship God when thousands of His images are struggling with poverty and disease in the same city? Is anything more antipodal to ideal humanity than the present distribution of wealth, and was there ever such an example of moral barrenness as the World War? Priests should tell us specifically how we reject the mercy and love of God. Has the woman who consults me as I write these lines, seeking relief from the suffering and incapacity imposed by shaking palsy, a disease which seems to be a reward of virtue, rejected them? She has borne and reared eight children; she has fed, clothed, and educated them from the proceeds of buttonhole-making; she has conformed to the teaching and ordinances of the Church in which she was born, baptized, and confirmed, and now she must submit to immobility and torture for ten or fifteen years unless she is fortunate enough to become hostess to some virulent germ.

How can we reconcile disease with the mercy and love of God? Do we not applaud man when he uses his intelligence to escape disease and prevent others from falling victim to it? Do we not accord the surgeon superhuman qualities when he boldly and dexterously cuts the body and removes disease that is seeking to destroy it? Is he not thwarting God's will? The matter really resolves itself into this: it is not a sin to use your intelligence about anything save God and religion.

To me, the popular conception of God is monstrous. It is alleged He is the perpetual fountain of love, the exhaustless source of mercy, the bottomless sea of compassion, and that justice has its origin and end in Him. But look where I may, I see naught but hatred, cruelty, selfishness, poverty, crime, suffering, and disease. How can these be reconciled with a kind, merciful, just God? The customary answer

is that it is not given to man to interpret or understand the ways of God, that poverty, hunger, tears,
and humiliation—the four beatitudes, according to
St. Luke—are vouchsafed us to insure salvation. We
are asked to believe that the road to true and everlasting happiness is love of poverty and suffering,
and then we devote ourselves with all our deter-
mination and strength to overcoming them; everyone
applauds us when we succeed and displays contempt
and scorn when we do not.

When God sends droughts and famine, earth-
quakes and floods, we are told we should implore
Him to alter His ways. It seems to me nothing
less than insult. If God is all-just and all-wise, and
He sees fit to devastate us with pestilence or destroy
us with war, we should accept supinely and resign-
edly His divine decisions. We do not accept them,
however. We utilize the means that science gives
us to prevent disease and disaster; we strive to tame
and discipline man's predatoriness and develop in
him justice and altruism that wars may be prevented;
we endeavor to forecast the heralds of what are
called calamities of nature.

In fact, we avail ourselves of every resource of
art and science to thwart what is said to be the will

of God, and our conduct gives us no concern; indeed, we boast of our accomplishment and just in proportion as success crowns our efforts in that direction, we maintain that we have advanced the welfare of the world and its peoples. And we are asked to believe that the calamities we are made to suffer are the ransom we pay for the sins of our forebears.

The rector of Trinity Church in New York has recently stated that we have ceased to be a Christian country and the Christian minority should not seek to enforce its standards on the un-Christian majority.

Where is the Christian minority and who constitutes it? Does it make one a Christian to be baptized or even confirmed? A Christian is one who lives or endeavors to live in conformity with Christ's mandates. But I have not encountered anyone who does it. Practically all of the pious Christians I have known were slaves to one or more of the deadly sins: pride, avarice, intemperance, lust, sloth, envy, or anger. I have neither seen nor heard anyone endeavoring to purge them save to suggest that they should be humble, generous, temperate, chaste, clean, content and serene.

The founder of the Christian religion decreed a

[241]

code of thought and conduct which may be sum-marized in a sentence, "Be ye therefore perfect, even as your Father which is in heaven is perfect." It is beyond man's capacity to be perfect or even to approximate perfection. The penalty of his impo-tency is punishment, punishment meted out in per-petuity after the body has ceased to be. We are told by those who claim the right to interpret Christ's teachings that endeavor to be perfect, and repent-ance for our transgressions, are adequate to obtain suspension of sentence and immunity; but repent-ance means foregoing all vain desires and satisfac-tions, pleasures, wealth, pride of life, and all that is summarized under the term duty to man and state. Not one individual in a million is capable of doing it. Fully to repent we have to forego things, and that is beyond our power to accomplish. We are asked to believe that we inherit a tendency to do wrong. Had not our remotest ancestors been so determined to make a hell upon earth for us, we might have escaped original sin. It was a great calamity to mankind that the teachings of Pelagius and his friend Cælestius were not accepted; they denied the racial consequences of Adam's fault, as-serted the entire innocence of the newborn, and recognized sinless men before the coming of Christ. The former stoutly contended that each man was responsible and liable to punishment only for his own acts, that divine grace is not necessary for human virtue, that it was within the capacity of every man to become virtuous by his own efforts. It is a calamity, too, that the teachings of Augustine prevailed against them, and particularly that Calvinism restored these teachings.

It is inconceivable that man should be the only product of nature that comes into being with a handicap. It is preposterous to maintain that our mothers conceived us in sin. They conceived us in love, in purity, and in beauty, and the gesture of conception is our closest link with God. To have associated the act of creation with sin is one of our greatest misfortunes.

Persons in mental distress who seek aid from me are forever talking about the sins they have committed, dwelling upon their unworthiness and proclaiming their doom. I do not know that the thoughts they have had and the acts they have done constitute sin, but when I submit a list of them to those who claim expert knowledge of the ways of

God, I am assured they are sinful. But the assurance does not convince me.

It is widely believed that when God made men in His image, He made them male and female that they might reproduce their kind. He endowed them with the genesic instinct, and the endowment was so generous and copious that few have been able to resist its demands.

Man has made it a sin to indulge or display that instinct save under stipulated conditions. The essence of the stipulation is marriage, which the Church has raised to the dignity of a sacrament.

The capacity to reproduce one's kind is given to the individual at about the fifteenth year of life. Marriage is neither prudent nor possible until approximately ten years later. During that period human beings must inhibit their genesic instinct. The male who does not succeed in doing so sins; and the female who fails not only sins, but is "ruined" as well. Should either seek and deliberately obtain vicarious satisfaction, they sin grievously. It is with the latter that I have largely to do. They are pitiful. This vicarious satisfaction is called "youthful sin," and, though not universal, it is well-nigh so. The majority treat it as an impostor, regret having indulged it, and forget it. The minority pigeonhole it in a compartment of their memory, from which, consciously or unconsciously, it escapes frequently and, flagrantly or surreptitiously, accuses the possessor. When the accusation is frank the accused feels himself a whited sepulcher; when it is camouflaged, a pariah; in both instances a sinner. Many women who have been brought up religiously magnify it into an unforgivable sin. The fear it engenders often disturbs the individual's life, disorders his mind, and thwarts self-realization.

There are many reasons why one should remain continent until he marries; all of them are good reasons. It is not a sin to be incontinent; it is bad taste, poor judgment, stupid management, an admission of inferiority and acceptance of defeat.

We know that the man and woman who can bring their creative possessions to their union undimmed, undefiled, with all their beauty and power, fragrance and freshness, will be rewarded by a feeling of dignity and satisfaction that self-control and overcoming of obstacles invariably engender.

We know that it makes for the welfare of the individual, the community, and the world for man to appease his creative urge within the confines of matrimony, and that should be sufficient reason. That he does not do so, and never has, is a matter for regret. That he cannot be induced to do so by threats of punishment hereafter has been proved conclusively. Greater success may follow from an appeal to his reason, self-respect, and sense of right.

Chastity is considered to be a virtue which leads us to abstain from unlawful pleasures of the flesh. Christian doctrine teaches us that there are three kinds: conjugal, the chastity of widowhood, and virginal. The first two are obligatory virtues because they render the flesh subject to the spirit, thus assuring to the faculties of the soul the possession of all their power, and to the body its vigor and its beauty. According to St. Augustine it is the only virtue that renders the mind of man pure enough to see God. The Roman Church teaches that the virtues of virginal chastity are profound peace and true liberty, the most perfect joys that the greatest victories can bestow and a magnificent reward in heaven. This seems to me an affront to God. If in His wisdom and omnipotence He had desired that His images should be chaste, he would have endowed them with the instinct of chastity instead of the instinct of creation.

Morality and decency will make epochal progress when men and women know how their bodies work; when no one will be ashamed of physiological functions; when no part of the body is considered indecent, and its actions abominable.

But this will never take place unless we liberate ourselves from religious hypocrisy, and we shall rid ourselves of that only by formulating a method of worshiping God that is consistent with man and nature.

We profess a religion which is at variance with science, intelligence, and reason, which no one practises, not even its priests, and which probably not one man in a thousand could practise, no matter how great its reward.

The Saviour of man said, "Woe unto you that are rich!" and our motivation from the day we become sentient is to create and enhance material possessions, and man and Church applaud in proportion as we succeed.

"Woe unto you that are full!" and every day anyone who has the means eats and drinks to satiety, and no one points the finger of scorn at him so long as his conduct does not outrage social convention or infract the laws of the state.

"Woe unto you that laugh, for you shall mourn and weep," and we regret every moment when the antecedent of laughter is denied us. We strive for diversion, amusement, happiness, and in proportion as we obtain them we are told that we lay up treasure in hell.

"Woe unto you when men shall bless you," and we exert ourselves strenuously and continuously to gain the esteem and approval of our fellows.

"The road to true and everlasting happiness is love of poverty and suffering." We hate poverty and the sole object of our activity would seem to be to overcome or escape it.

We are told to do that which it is impossible for us to do—to love suffering. When we encounter an individual who gets pleasure from having pain inflicted upon him, we call him a masochist, a monster, and a degenerate. In a lifetime of intimacy with sufferers I have not met one who loved it.

Scan as I may the road to everlasting happiness I see no advocates of the divine law or expositors of religion devoted to poverty. I see them living in comfort, luxury even, traveling in private cars or palatial yachts, clothing themselves in rich raiment, fraternizing with mammon, serenading the opulent, caterwauling the materially exalted, and struggling for preferment.

The affirmation that the welfare of the soul is enhanced by humiliating, denying, and punishing the body has its foundation in fanaticism. A healthy soul is the complement of a healthy body, and *vice versa*. There is nothing so salutary to a healthy mind as a healthy body, and the body cannot remain healthy if it is humiliated, hampered, and harassed.

"Take no thought for your life, what ye shall eat, or what ye shall drink, nor yet for your body, what ye shall put on."

Yet, from the moment our children become capable of feeling and thinking we tell them that life's demands are to be provident, productive, and prudent. We tell our youths that they must put something aside for rainy days, make provision for the time when they can no longer toil, that they may be able to discharge obligations, and above all that they may merit the esteem of their fellows and receive their approbation. It is of the things that we are admonished to take no thought, and one other, that we think continuously from the time we are endowed with the capacity for constructive thought to the day we are deprived of it by age or

[249]

death. We are told not to lay up for ourselves treasures upon earth, but should we not attempt to do so we are looked upon as wastrels, and should we not succeed, we are considered failures. When we succeed, and donate some of it to bishops determined to perpetuate their names by building cathedrals, and to missions for the conversion and salvation of heathens, we are assured that we effect a transfer of the treasure from earth to heaven. And though the nucleus of the treasure be from robbing widows, defrauding orphans, crushing competitors, fleecing the unwary, the honorable amend is made by donating part of it to "the Church."

When we decide to move a house we do not say to a child, "Pick up that building and deposit it upon that hill." He is as capable of doing it as he is of loving his enemies, of blessing them that curse him, of doing good to them who hate him, and praying for those who persecute him.

Why profess a religion that cannot be practised? Why not have one that is consonant with man's capacity? Assuming that God made man and that life on earth is a preparation for life in paradise; that the soul is a reality and not a figment of man's fears, selfishness, and egotism; that immortality is a wage to be earned, not a gift to be accepted—it is incredible that a task beyond his capacity, a problem beyond his power of solution, should be imposed upon him.

It may be said that He who was the Son of Man lived in accordance with the rules that He framed for man's guidance. He did, and his fellow men taunted, pursued, persecuted, and crucified Him, and it is likely that is what men would do today to one who would attempt to walk in His footsteps.

It has been said many times that anyone who should attempt to put in operation the whole of the Christian religion would be locked up as a lunatic. But even though it were in our power to imagine a man who would do exactly what it teaches without being committed, we should be confronted with the personification of a monster. He would forsake his family, rob them of the fruit of his or their labor, be a constant source of offense to decency, without regard for all civic duties, an outcast and a pariah.

We are told that God created the world of His own free choice, out of nothing, made men in His own image—male and female—blessed them and gave them two commands, "Be fruitful and multiply, replenish the earth and subdue it."

Scarcely had they begun to make effective His commands than He thrust upon them, through the medium of one of the things that creepeth upon the earth over which they were given dominion—to wit, the serpent—a handicap they could never surmount. They were given no opportunity for repentance or reform; no mercy was shown them; they were sentenced immediately and the sentence was binding upon their descendants even unto the present day and it shall continue forever.

After having allowed them to serve it for millions of years, He decreed to restore man to his original state and determined to accomplish this reconciliation in such a way as to satisfy justice. He promised a redeemer who, in man's stead, was to render full satisfaction for the offense committed against Him. This redeemer was to restore to man the sanctifying grace and the hope of supernatural bliss forfeited by his sin.

Finally, He sent His Son to restore the heritage that Adam had lost, and allowed Him to be humiliated, tortured, and crucified.

Christ, it is said, ransomed mankind, "He washed us from our sins by His blood." By this ransom, He satisfied the divine justice, delivered us from sin and eternal damnation, and purchased for us the goods lost by sin.

Thus, we are confronted with the paradoxical situation of deriving our most admirable impulses and most elevating inspiration from one of the most cruel and inhuman of teachings: that vicarious sacrifice and monstrous tortures have redeemed us and purged us of sin.

Why not have a religion that harmonizes with the knowledge and thought that is vouchsafed us? It is absurd to say that religion is immutable; it has been subject to as many mutations as science itself. We say that love is the great solvent of the world, and yet we frighten our children with monstrous doctrines about heaven and hell. Threats of punishment, possibly, may direct or influence some to righteousness better than any other kind of teaching, but I have never met any who were benefited by it.

Why not have a religion that is practicable and in conformity with science? It is farthest from me to underestimate the value of religious emotion. It is ennobling and purifying, and I am sure that religion is essential to mankind. Its code of social hygiene goes far to check disease and keep man sane. Its

moral censorship diminishes vices and prevents excesses whose tendency is to destroy the individual or
the race. But why not have a religion that is based
upon a system of ethics that is plausible and work-
able, to which the best of men can live up?

I am quite aware of the sense of futility which
accompanies an effort at expressing views which, to
some, may appear as an attack upon organized and
accepted religion. Man's spirit needs religion as his
body needs bread and oxygen. His spiritual life,
his higher instincts, his sense of morality, are all
dependent upon the religious training he receives,
whether or not he be conscious of it. And to dare
attempt a reversal of the established order, one must
have something to put in its stead, something better,
more efficacious, less offensive to reason and sense.

I maintain that none of the people of the Western
civilization, whatever their creed, have evolved a
satisfactory religion—that is, one which satisfies at
once that enigmatic possession called the soul and
that complex organism the mind. The religion of
today, when it conforms to the laws of sanctity,
offends those of nature, and there seems no reconciliation possible between it and science. Were men
to believe the truth of the assertion that "God, who

is the final reason for everything, is the scientific explanation of nothing," and make an effort to submit their emotions to their intellect, religion as it is understood today would no longer be acceptable in its present form; the same religion, adapted to fit the ever-changing process of civilization, might be retained, but the spirit and the letter of its tenets would both be changed.